Zills:

Music on Your Fingertips
All About Finger Cymbals

Best on Drum & Costuming [signature]

Enjoy!
Aloah Westerfeld

Best Zills & Thrills,
George Goncalves

Other Books
By Dawn Devine ~ Davina

Becoming a Belly Dancer: From Student to Stage
with Sara Shrapnell, Alisha Westerfeld, and Poppy Maya

The Cloth of Egypt: All About Assiut
with Alisha Westerfeld

Embellished Bras
with Barry Brown

Bedlah, Baubles, & Beads
with Barry Brown

From Turban to Toe Ring
with Barry Brown

Costuming From the Hip
with Barry Brown

Skirting the Issues & Pants for the Dance

Hints & Tips for the Belly Dance Costumer

Zills

Music On Your Fingertips
All About Finger Cymbals

By Dawn Devine
Photos by Alisha Westerfeld
Illustrations by George Goncalves

Ibexa Press
2016

Text by Dawn Devine ~ Davina
Photos by Alisha Westerfeld
Illustrations by George Goncalves
Additional photos by Michael Baxter

Editing by:
    Joe Engledow
    Nancy Hay
    Michael Hyde
    Chris Schoedel

Production:
    Jerry Case

Dawn Devine
Ibexa Press
© 2016

In memory of

Harry Saroyan

The King of Zills

Table of Contents

Preface

Hello, I'm Davina aka Dawn Devine, and welcome to my zill book! When I began researching the history of finger cymbals within culture and dance, I didn't realize how scant the historical record was surrounding the origins and historical use of zills. My interest in exploring the roots of zill playing began when I was in graduate school studying art history. It was one particular painting, "Dance of the Almeh" by Jean-Léon Gérôme in 1863 that caught my attention. It got me started musing about zills, more specifically, when they became intimately enmeshed with the art of Middle Eastern belly dance.

Gérôme's painting inspired a series of significant research papers, leading me to deeply explore European Orientalism. My focus was on the trope of the dance figure in Orientalist paintings and the iconography of the Middle Eastern dancer within the greater scope of Western art. For mid-19th-century viewers, these paintings, and others like it, sharpened the taste for Middle Eastern travel; seeing a dance performance when on holiday became an expected part of every tourist itinerary.

However, what captured my mind and drew my focus was her finger cymbals. This painting serves as a historical document that dates zill playing to 1863. By including the zills in the painting, a detail that Gérôme could have easily chosen to leave out, we, the viewers, are sent a message - that these finger cymbals are important and integral to the dance. Although the scenario appears to be one of total fantasy, as a practicing belly dancer, I see authenticity of the dancer in a signature pose with arms held aloft. But most impressive all is Gérôme's level of detail. I knew that he had seen an authentic performer from the lovely hands and fingers, accurately painted with zills worn on middle finger and thumb. After this epiphany, I began a life-long quest to trace back the history of finger cymbals as they are depicted in art.

My hunt took a slight turn in 2005, when I first visited Paris and spotted ancient Egyptian finger cymbals on display in the Louvre. They were presented as part of the thematic displays of religious and everyday artifacts, tiny by comparison to the epic temple facades and gigantic sarcophagi. In these display cases, small items used by Egyptians in everyday life were presented with care and grouped by context. Although the jewelry section dazzled me, it was the displays devoted to music that drew my rapt attention. In these exhibits, ancient musical instruments were presented including sistrums, harps, flutes, tambourines, clappers, and finger cymbals. Although there is, as of now, no place where ancient Egyptian dancers are depicted wearing finger cymbals, it is clear that they were used to produce music, and were considered important enough by the Egyptians to have been placed in their tombs to take along into the next life. At this point, my research took a leap backwards in time, and I left the world of painting and began a search for finger cymbals used in antiquity.

So after years of research and decades of dance, I'm pleased to share my research and experience with you. It is my hope that you will find this publication informative and inspirational.

Best of luck and happy dancing!

Dawn Devine ~ Davina

Introduction

Zills really are music on your fingertips. Donning a set of finger cymbals and performing with them lifts a dancer to higher level of proficiency within the art of belly dance. When you play zills, you transform yourself into a musician, demonstrating your mastery of the music by interacting with a live band or reinterpreting a recorded composition. The familiar jingling ring of finger cymbals are one of the hallmarks of the belly dancer. When you think of a belly dancer, your mind might envision a performer exploding from backstage at a formal concert with arms held high, cymbals jingling a hello to the audience, slinking through a crowded restaurant with zills ringing, or dancing through a market or fair with her finger cymbals her only musical accompaniment.

Finger cymbals are known by a variety of names. In Turkey, they are called zill as a single unit, and ziller as a plural, while in the US, the anglicized plural term is zills. In Egyptian Arabic, they are known as sagat, and you can tell where a dancer learned her finger cymbal work based on what she calls her instruments. Throughout this book, we use these three terms, zills, sagat and finger cymbals, interchangeably. A "set" of finger cymbals is composed of two pairs, or four total. They are worn on the tips of the middle finger and the thumb, over the base of the fingernail. There are a wide variety of sizes, shapes, metals, and they come in one-hole or two-holed varieties. But no matter what style you choose, or what you call them, they have been an essential component of the professional belly dancer's repertoire.

Many dancers believe that zill-work may be a dying art, slowly passing into the history of Middle Eastern belly dance. Finger cymbals were once an integral part of every dancer's performance, and part of the long tradition of our art form. Quality zill work was a point of pride and a hallmark of achievement and professionalism and even today, is a required skill for performing in nightclubs and restaurants.

There are many factors contributing to the apparent loss of zill skills among performing dancers.

Egyptian dance stars are performing less frequently with sagat. Celebrity belly dancers have grown to rely on the finger cymbal player in their band or orchestra to supply the classic high-toned tinkling accompaniment. Professional performers have focused on developing a signature styles, working with complex props, and honing their dance skills, leaving zill playing to professional musicians.

In the US, there are a number of factors that have contributed to the decline of zill playing. Many working performers follow the lead of their Egyptian dance icons, and leave the finger cymbals to one of the musicians, or to select recorded music with a strong zill component. As finger cymbals have fallen out of favor amongst hobbyists and semi-pros, new students of the dance now face difficulties locating instructors who teach zill playing. Without zill playing icons to look up to, there is

Teachers are abandoning cymbal work instruction for a variety of personal and professional reasons. Some teachers, to facilitate quick turnaround from beginner to performing dancer, have streamlined their curriculum and eliminated finger cymbal instruction. Some instructors simply don't want to add the complexity of teaching dance technique and musicianship until more advanced classes, at levels where there are fewer dedicated students. Many instructors simply don't feel competent teaching zill playing because they themselves don't utilize finger cymbals in their own performance repertoire.

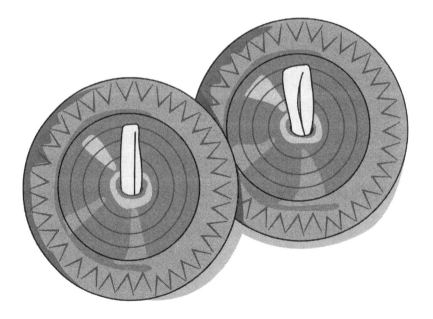

Many dance instructors from around the globe include finger cymbal instruction as part of their core training. Malia of San Francisco Bay Area is renowned for her skill at both teaching finger cymbals and playing them in performance. Illustration by George Goncalves from an original photo by Alisha Westerfeld

Many new students of belly dance consider zill playing to be the hardest part of learning this dance art, and simply decide that playing finger cymbals is not necessary for their personal enjoyment of this hobby. In addition, over the past twenty years, there has been a tremendous development of alternative and fusion styles of dance. These artistic explorations of western music and fusion musical compositions, with non Middle Eastern based rhythm patterns, may not lend themselves to finger cymbal accompaniment. The abundance of recorded music that includes zills in the instrumentation has increased. In addtion, students of dance have found they can greatly reduce their stress levels by eliminating the pressure of playing finger cymbals at recitals and student shows.

All of these factors have played into the decline of zill-playing among today's dancers. And yet, playing finger cymbals is one of the hallmarks of this dance form and, perhaps, the most distinctive feature, one that separates belly dance from all other styles of folk-dance. This book is designed to provide key historical information, details about the construction of various styles of finger cymbals, approaches to playing zills, and a dictionary of the rhythms and patterns used by today's performers.

Let's face it, it is impossible to learn to play finger cymbals from a book. Seek out professional dancers and teachers to take group classes, workshops, and private lessons with to learn to play. If you don't have access to in-person instruction, invest in a quality video instructional, or take distance classes with a zill master. Use this reference guide as an enhancement to your practice, to bring you greater knowledge and understanding of finger cymbals as an instrument, and to help you take your zill playing to the next level.

Continuing History

At some fundamental level, finger cymbals are about freedom and power for the belly dancer. With a set of zills, a dancer can perform anytime and anyplace, without need for a band or boom box. It was only in the last 150 years that sound recordings could replicate and replace the presence of live music. Before that, music was special; it required a group of people to come together and perform. But if our ancient dance-sisters were anything like you and I, they certainly craved the freedom to perform at will.

The moment when zill playing entered the history of Middle Eastern belly dance is unknown. Though many musical and dance scholars have theorized about the origins of this dance, ultimately, we simply don't have the information. However, what we do have is 2000 years of historical record, in which dance has played a small part. Dancers appear in paintings of court life. Travelers recorded tales of seeing Oriental dance while exploring the world.

Because belly dance is folk dance, it has been accepted as a cultural staple by its own practitioners. Dance is a process that doesn't need to be analyzed or recorded because it is as intrinsic to life as breathing and eating. The steps and moves developed regional flare, and were passed from dancer to dancer organically without text book or codified language. Belly dance is at once sacred and profane, a performance art brought to life by people for people.

It is only in the last 50 years that scholarship in Middle Eastern dance began in earnest, and with few scholars and so much unwritten history, it will take decades before this art form develops a uniform vocabulary. In the meantime, dance teachers do their best to communicate the names of moves, with a combination of traditional names and physical descriptions.

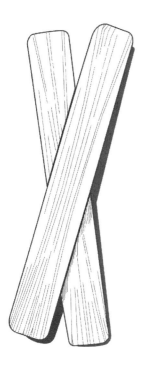

Tapping two wooden objects together to make a resonate sound pre-dates the invention of writing and pairs of playing sticks appear in the grave goods of peoples from around the globe. This pair of modern 'wooden bones" is contemporary equivalent that's used in school classrooms today to help childeren learn about rhythm and tempo.

Bronze Zills

Cymbals reach back into the very dawn of time, coming from the early bronze era pre-dating literate culture. Greeks referred to cymbals as kumbalon while the Romans knew them as cymbala, plural for cymbalum. When they begin to appear in the arts and writings of early civilizations, cymbals are most often associated with rituals, religious worship, royalty and the military. Hand-held percussion instruments used while dancing have been a part of the human experience, and continues to be used not only in Middle Eastern belly dance, but in other folk dances around the world.

Examples of finger cymbals pre-date the development of written language by several millennium. The copper age or Chalcolithic, begins around 7500 BCE, the age of the earliest copper smelting works. In antiquity, metal was a precious commodity, so it was reused over and over again so there are few metal artifacts remaining from this period. Copper items have been found in ancient burials world-wide and include small items such as jewelry, tiny sculptures, and small hand tools. So far, no copper finger cymbals have been discovered and entered into the historic record.

The bronze era is heralded in by a paradigm shift in technology. Bronze, an alloy of copper and tin, was much stronger than pure copper, and allowed for innovations in tool making that lead to both better farming implements and more dangerous weapons of war. Although the bronze age began in various parts of the world at different times, the bronze era around the Mediterranean started at about 3700 BCE and lasted until approximately 500 BCE. During this time, mankind made many leaps including the development of writing and the rise of major cities and civilizations.

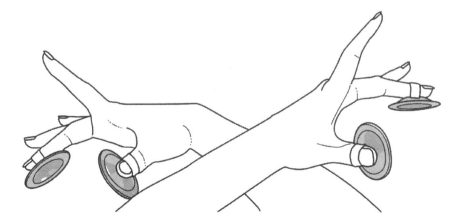

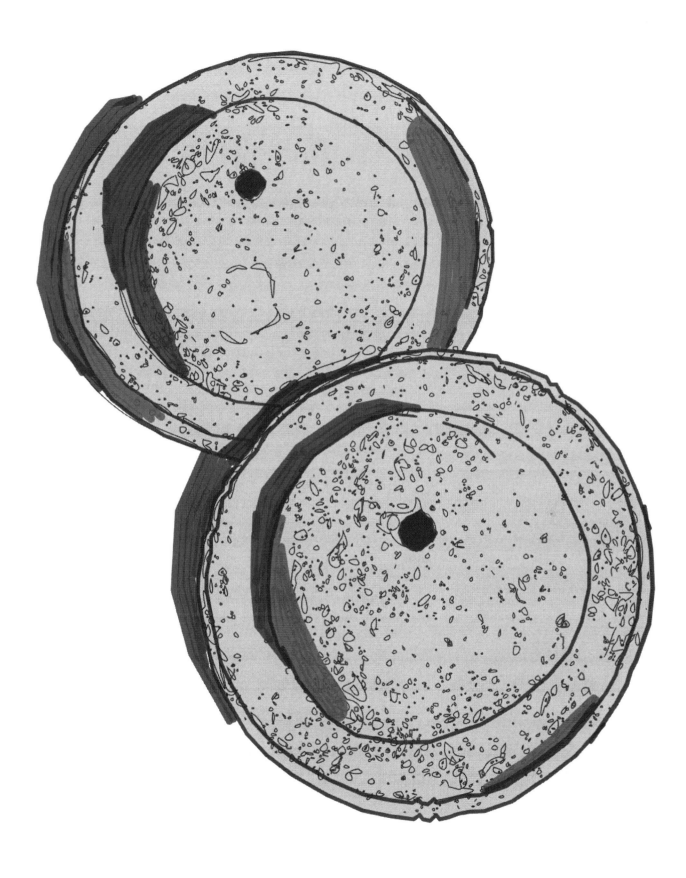

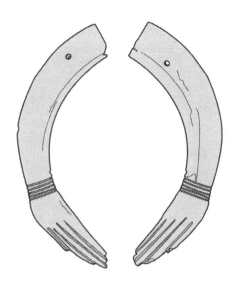

Ancient Eygpt

Finger cymbals in pairs and sets of four, have been excavated from burials around the Mediterranean from Italy and Greece, through the levant, and across North Africa. Examples of bronze finger cymbals date as far back as the ancient Greek archaic period and to the early dynastic period in Egypt.

Many different styles of clappers, shakers, and rattles were placed in the tombs of Egyptian people. Clappers made of bone in the shapes of hands are found throughout the region in virtually every era. The pair at left are redrawn from a set approximately 5" long and made from ivory on display at the Louvre, Paris France.

Egyptian finger cymbals made from bronze are also fairly common. Pairs and sets of four have found their way to museum antiquities collections around the globe. The pair of finger cymbals below left are currently on display at the Louvre in Paris, France.

When musuem visitors look into the cases at ancient finger cymbals, they are often struck by how modern they look. Bronze resists corrosion and many finger cymbals have really stood the test of time, maintaining their original shape and size. Although we modern humans might be bigger, our hands haven't changed much, so zills 4 millenia old are much the same configuration as those today.

Bronze sistrum were used in religious celebrations along with finger cymbals and clappers. These metal rattles are often made with a U-shaped frame attached to a handle. Holes on either side of the U-shape would hold metal rods that would rattle in their holes. Sistra are made out of bronze, or faience, a blue-green colored ceramic.

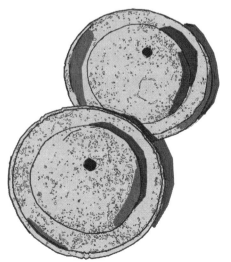

Rattles of this type are found throughout the ancient world, and were used by the Minoan culture and later by the Greeks. Dancers wishing to create their own band will often pick up hand-held percussion instruments like rattles and shakers to create fill for the dominant zill.

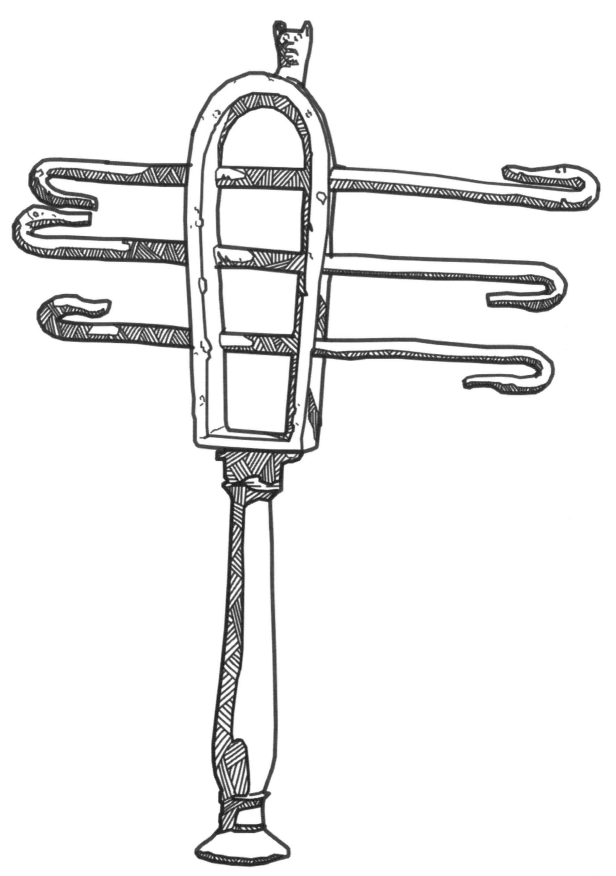

Finger Cymbals in Turkey

Turkey gained fame as a major producer of high-quality cymbals. Our current term, zill, comes from the renowned Armenian alchemist Avedis who worked in Constantinople in the first quarter of the 17th century. The high quality of his cymbals were noticed by Sultan Osman II, who paid Avedis lavishly in gold and then named him Zildgian, which means "cymbal smith" in Armenian. The Zildgian company, founded by Avedis himself, dates to 1623 and continues to be one of the world leaders in cymbal production, including orchestra quality cast-bronze finger cymbals.

Throughout the 18th and 19th century, numerous representations of dancers with arms held aloft and cymbals on their fingers underscore the close association between oriental dancing and zills. Orientalist painters, fascinated by this folk dance art, chose dancers as a figural motif and often captured their characteristic poses and props, including zills.

Today, finger cymbals are available at every price point, in a variety of shapes and sizes and metal compositions to suit the needs of every dancer. There are several American companies that specialize in musically tuned performance zills designed for dancers, which are available in a variety of sizes, metallic finishes and decorative stamped patterns.

Three pairs of modern bronze zills made using ancient casting methods. The sets on the top and lower right are from the Zildjian company. The set on the bottom left are made from a B8 formula from Sabian. Both of these companies are run by members of the Turkish Zildjian clan who have been making cymbals for over 400 years.

Concussion Idiophones

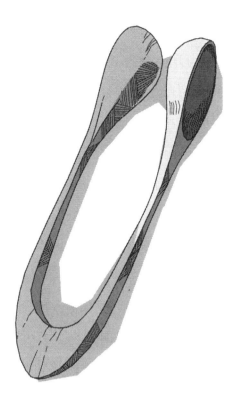

Finger cymbals are part of the larger group of instruments classified as idiophones. These are instruments made from materials that are naturally resonant, creating their musical tone from their intrinsic properties. Finger cymbals fall into the subcategory of concussion idiophones, where the notes are made by striking two items together; both vibrate to make a pleasing sound. In constrast, percussion idiophones are struck with a non-reverberating object like a stick or mallet to create a single vibrating tone. Examples of percussion idiophones include the xylophone, gongs, and cowbells.

Concussion idiophones are used throughout a wide variety of folk dance styles including the castanets of Spanish folk dancer, the spoons of Turkish and Central Asian folk dancing. However, not every instrument of this style is used exclusively for dancing. Instruments like the spoons top left require both hands to play, and are used primarily as percussion by musicians in a group or band setting.

Above, percussion instrumetns derived from spoons are popular around the world, but are not used for dancing. Below, Tibetan tingsha are used in service to religious rites and in meditiation practices.

24

Turkish Spoons

The Turkish spoon dance, known as oyunu havasi or kasik oyunu in Turkish or chorus koutalia in Greek, is a regional folk dance performed throughout Turkey, but most closely associated with the region around the city of Konya. This dance was already being performed in the Byzantine era, and sets of dancing spoons have been found in burial goods. Turkish spoons are played by both male and female performers socially during line dances that include simple steps, knee driven kicks, and complicated footwork patterns. On stage, the dance becomes more stylized with complex choreography and more dramatic leaps, jumps, and kicks.

A set of Turkish dancing spoons is composed of four identical spoons. Each hand holds two spoons, one between the thumb and index finger, and the other between the pointer and middle finger. The roundness of the bowls of the spoons are held together. The performer opens their hands and then closes them quickly, striking the bowls together to make a clacking sound. The speed of the hand movements and the tightness of the grip impact the quality of the sound.

Turkish dancing spoons come in a variety of styles including those with short and long handles. They are often highly ornate with decorations burned, etched, or simply painted onto the wooden surface.

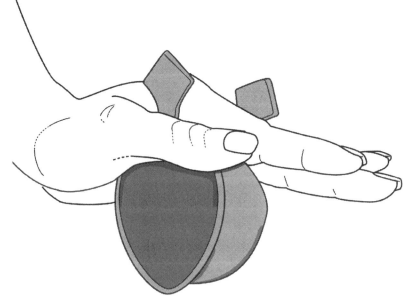

Spanish Castanets

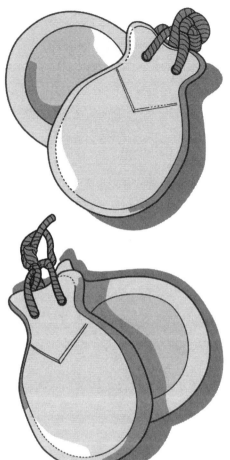

Wooden castanets have long been associated with traditional Andalusian folk dancing. Historians theorize that clappers arrived with the Greeks more than two thousand years ago. Castanets are traditionally made from wood, though historically, they were also made from ivory or metal. The word castanet originates from the Spanish word Catalina, or "chestnut." They are also called pulgaretes, derived from the Spanish word pulgar or "thumb" or are called platillos, Spanish for "saucer." Wood is the most common material used today, though modern examples are often made from sturdy resin.

The Gitana, or Iberian Roma, integrated the castanet into their traditional dances, such as the Zambra and for siguiriyas. Mainstream Spanish use the castanets as well, performing the "Sevillanas" with the instrument's accompaniment. Castanets come in pairs, and dancers and musicians play two pairs. The instruments are tied together with a string or rope that not only holds the pair together, but also to hold the castanets on the thumb.

When playing the castanets, the performer holds one side cupped loosely in the palm of their hand. The loose castanet is tapped with the fingers to create the signature sound. Traditionally, the dominant hand plays sharply staccato quick clicking tones, tapping with fingertips in quick succession. The non-dominant hand plays a base rhythm that keeps the tempo and serves as a sonic anchor for the complexity of the other castanet.

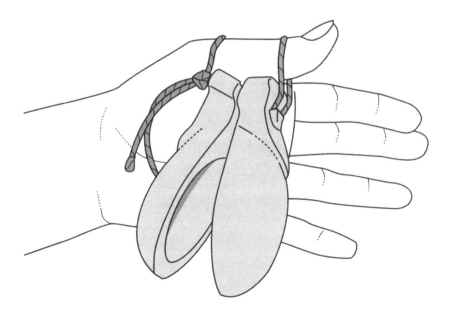

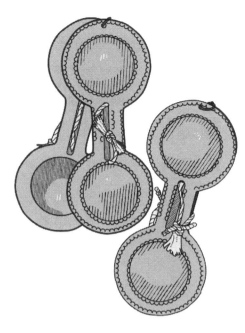

Moroccan Qarkabeb

Like the other concussive idiophones, the Qarkabeb is an instrument played by ethnic Berber Gnawa musical groups. Folkloric tradition holds that these flattened dumbbell-shaped metal clappers were invented by sub-Saharan slaves that were brought to the Maghreb region. The shape related to the shackles that held their ankles, and the tinny, clacking sound echoed the sound of the metal chains that bound them in place. The rhythm is said to echo the sound of horses' hooves, as the young men were gathered up and dragged into slavery.

Gnawa musicians carry on these traditions, performing their almost hypnotic music combined with a stylized spinning of large tassels worn on the head. Often a musical group will include an acrobatic dancer who adds a visual dimension, but typically, the Qarkabeb player is a band member.

These are played in groups along with a skin-covered four-string guitar called a guimbri and a large double-headed barrel drum called a tbel.

Today's Qarkabeb are made from iron or steel, and come in a variety of lengths. A set is four, composed of two pairs that are held together at one end by a string or a metal ring. Rope strings are looped through the neck of the clappers, and the fingers and thumb slip under these loops and hold the instrument during play.

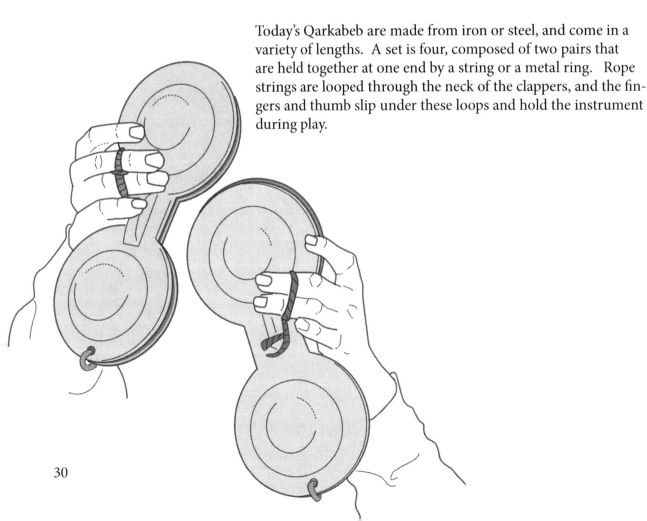

Construction & Manufacture

Before we discuss how finger cymbals are played by belly dancers, let's take a moment to consider what finger cymbals are, what they are made of, and how they are constructed.

Many performers who play finger cymbals when they dance take them for granted. They simply buy what is available. They might make that choice based on recommendations, and on how appealing they look and sound. But most dancers may not be aware of what metal their finger cymbals are made from, or how they came to be.

In the following pages, we will present information on the main metals and methods used for making performance grade finger cymbals,

One Hole or Two?
Traditional zills have a single hole placed at the top of the bell. Ribbon or elastic is threaded through the hole, and held in place on the underside inside the bell with a large knot.

Modern zills come with a two hole or slit configuration which allows the elastic to be threaded through the metal, cut and stitched to make a comfortable low-profile loop.

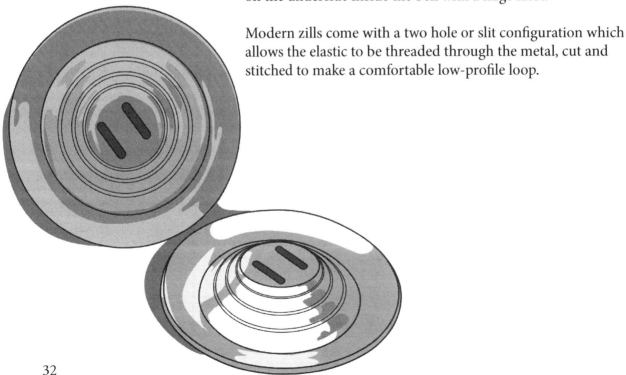

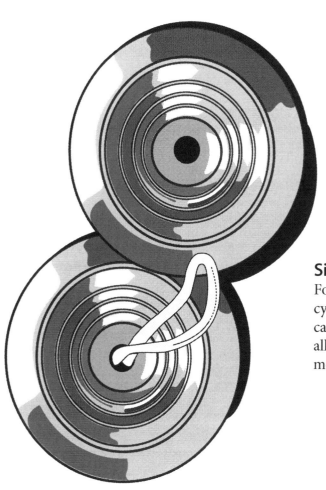

Single Holed Zills

For most of the history of humankind, finger cymbals were made of bronze using the sand cast method. Prior to the industrial revolution, all zills, sagat, and cengi were made of cast metals with a single hole.

Double Slotted Zills

During the industrial revolution, techniques for working with metal improved. Great strides were made in all aspects of metallurgy, and the tools and techniques used for industry made it possible to improve the sound and look of musical instruments. With the advent of the industrial press, a double slotted construction was possible, and became a prefered style for dancers who enjoy the control that a double-slot style provides.

Metals & Materials

Zills, like all cymbals, are traditionally made from a group of metals known "red metals" in the industrial world. These are a family of alloys that utilize copper as the base metal, and includes bronze, brass, and german silver. Major manufacturers keep their precise metal compositions secret. But in general The four most common red metals used for instruments include the following.

Copper

Pure copper zills are rarely made because of the softness of the metal and their tendency to turn green. Copper cores are often used as a base for plating, which can muddy the sound.

Modern Bronze

An alloy of copper and tin, bronze will often have dullish pink color. Primarily used today for creating fine sculpture, bronze has an intrinsic ring and large bells are often made using the classic "bell bronze" ratio of 80% copper and 20% tin.

Brass

Today's modern highquality zills are mostly made from brass. This is a mixture of 60% copper and 40% zinc, often with additional metals added in to create "secret recipes." Brass is highly maliable, and easy to work with, but becomes hard, so retains it's shape even under the punnishment of frequent playing.

German Silver

Invented in the 19th century, German silver is an alloy that is a mixture of 60% copper, 20% zinc,, and 20% nickle. This metal is often called "Nickle Brass" or "Nickle Silver" and can sometimes have low quantities of actual silver in the mix depending on the manufacturer. It has a bright durable finish that makes it perfect for use in instruments like flutes and picolos, trumpets, and for finger cymbals.

Mystery Metal

Cheaper zills tend to be made from lower quality mystery metal. When purchasing finger cymbals look for quality ingredients like bronze, brass, and German silver. These metals have proven to have long track record of providing beautiful musical tone and durability. If says "brass toned" remember, that refers to the way it looks, not necessarily how it will sound.

New materials such as plastic and wood, like the set below, are now being made into zills for practice and for a totally different and unique sound.

Cast Cymbals

The oldest method for crafting a set of cymbals is the sand casting method, in which molten metal is poured into a mold made of or lined with sand. This method creates a zill with a rough finish and a deep rich tone. Cast cymbals are generally made with a single hole at the top due to the technological limitiations of working with molten bronze.

Ancient cymbals were often made using the recipe B20, or an alloy of 80% copper and 20% tin with traces of silver added to fine tune the blend. The highest quality cymbals for modern drum kits and marching bands are still made from the basic B20 formula, though the recipe used to create each alloy varies from company to company and are closely guarded trade secrets.

The finger cymbals opposite are made with a variation on the B8 recipe, where the ratio is 92% copper to 8% tin. This recipe is used to create highly resonant cymbals and is favored by many modern drum-kit players for it's strength and durability.

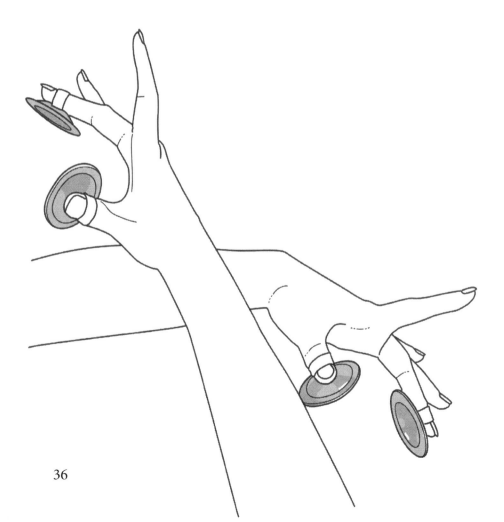

Construction Methods

Over the many centuries of finger cymbal production, makers of musical instruments have experimented with differnt metals, shapes, and manufacturing technques. The following is a list of the four most common styles of creating the shape of the zill. Once the ingot or casting is made, they are heated and then, while hot, are rolled to press it thin layers. The cymbals are then cut from the metal and then hand worked to create their unique sound. Here are the three methods used to create the shape of the cymbal, and all three method can appear in some

Hammering

Hammered cymbals are still made, and are consdiered by many musicians to be the top of the line instruments. Large cymbals have their bell pressed into the center, and then are hammered from the edge of the bell, accross the rim to the lip. Each tap of the hammer works together to tune the metal to create the perfect pitch and tone. Unfortunately, it's difficult to get hand hammered finger cymbals today.

Lathing

In this manufcaturing method, the cymbal is placed on a spinning lathe and tools are used to remove material from the blank to create the shape of the rim. This method leaves behind characteristic groves that impact the sound of the final instrument. Often lathed cymbals are hand hammered into final shape to give the ultimate preciion and perfection of the final tone of the instrument.

Stamping and pressing

Most contemporary zill producers use a stamping method to produce their insturments. This production technique begins with sheet metal, often in strips or rolls, from which the cymbal blanks are cut out and pressed into shape using industrial presses.

Tradtional cast bronze finger cymbals have a characteristic rough surface that is part of their charm. Notice the color tone and surface appearance of the finger cymbal above right from the Zildjian cymbal. Their press made cousins can be polished to a highly reflective shine like the bronze zill from Saroyan Mastercrafts to the left.

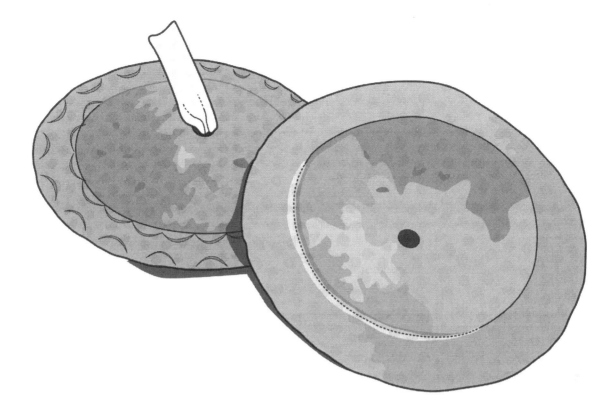

Above: Hammered zills have been traditionally made from working hot metal with hammers to get the perfect shape. Hand hammering is still used today for manufacturing large high quality cymbals used in drum kits. Hammering leaves an irregular dimpled pattern.

Below: A post industrial revolution method for making cymbals includes spinning on a lathe and griding away material to reach the targeted shape of the cymabals. This creates a characteristic spiral line on the surface of the cymbal.

Modern Manufacturing

Today's highest quality zills are created using precision machining techniques. In a visit to the Saroyan Mastercrafts factory in Riverside California, we were introduced to the multi-step process they use to hand craft their professional quality musical instruments. The current owners Vincent and Virginia Fesunoff offer informative tours of their company, and Vincent broke down their manufacturing process into four main steps.

Their finger cymbals begin as coiled flat metal made from serval proprietary alloys for their different models. The bulk of their finely tuned instruments are made from brass. Several models are also offered in high-quality bronze and German silver.

Each set of finger cymbals is hand machined either using a traditional fly-wheel industrial press, or on a modern CNC machine. Each zill is made using four dies. The first punches a flat disk from the metal and determines the diameter of the finished zill. The second die embosses a pattern or design into the surface of the zill. Giving each model it's own distinct look. The third die is composed of two parts, a top and bottom, that form the shape or profile of the cymbal. The fourth die punches two slots at the top of the bell for threading the elastic.

Once the set of zills have been stamped out, embossed, shaped, and slotted, they await their multiple passes through a polishing machine that creates the mirror-like reflective surface that is one of the hallmarks of Saroyan finger cymbals.

Not all finger cymbals are created equal. When shopping for your next set, be sure totest the quality of the metal, which you can hear in the tone or voice of the instruments.. Look for clean and well executed embossing with clean distinct lines. The surface should be polished and clean from defects. Always try to buy the best quality finger cymbals you can afford to have a life-time of quality play.

Saroyan Mastercrafts offers more than 50 styles of finger cymbals from tiny mini zills sized for the smallest hands, to orchestral quality finger cymbals for professional procussionists.

Left: After a blank is punched, the second step is to emboss the zill with a pattern. Notice the clarity of the lines in this design.

Below: After embossing, the finger cymbal is pressed into shape. It's at this stage when the dimensions of the bell and the shape of the profile are pressed into place.

Left: Once the double-slots have been punched into the top of the finger cymbal, it will go through a multi-step polishing process until it shines like the two examples on the opposite page.

Zill Anatomy

Finger cymbals are made following a traditional shape. No matter if you buy inexpensive zills from a discount provider, or high-quality orchestra grade instruments, your finger cymbals will follow a standard format. Variations in these characteristics will effect the quality of the sound produced by the instruments.

Bell or Cup – The domed area at the center of the zill which shapes the quality of the ring tone.

Profile or Bow – The curvature of the cymbal from the bell to the edge, which affects the pitch. The higher and more dome-shaped the bell, the higher the pitch of the ring.

Taper – The change in thickness of the metal from the center hole to the edge. Thicker zills tend to be of lower tone, while zills that taper to very thin edges can create a delicate tone, but also are physically more delicate.

Rim or Lip – The characteristic flat striking edge of finger cymbals. Broader flatter rims will create a louder "clapping" sound when hit face-to-face.

Size – is measured across the diameter. Simply put, the bigger the zill, the louder they will be.

Weight – The weight will affect the overall pitch and tone. Heavier zills will have a cleaner brighter sound, while lighter weight zills generally have a thinner higher ring tone.

Opposite - Four of the most common shapes of finger cymbals.

A - **Domed cast zills** - the distinction between the rim and the bell is distinct, but not sharp.

B - **Flipped rim** - In this style, popular in Turkey, the bell is more straight sided, with a turned up rim.

C - **Flared** - This finger cymbal has a smooth flared shape with a distinct, but not sharp turn of the lip.

D - **Domed** - This is probably the most common shape, with a distinct rounded bell, and a distinct bend into the rim.

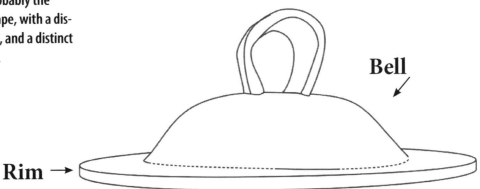

Bell

Rim →

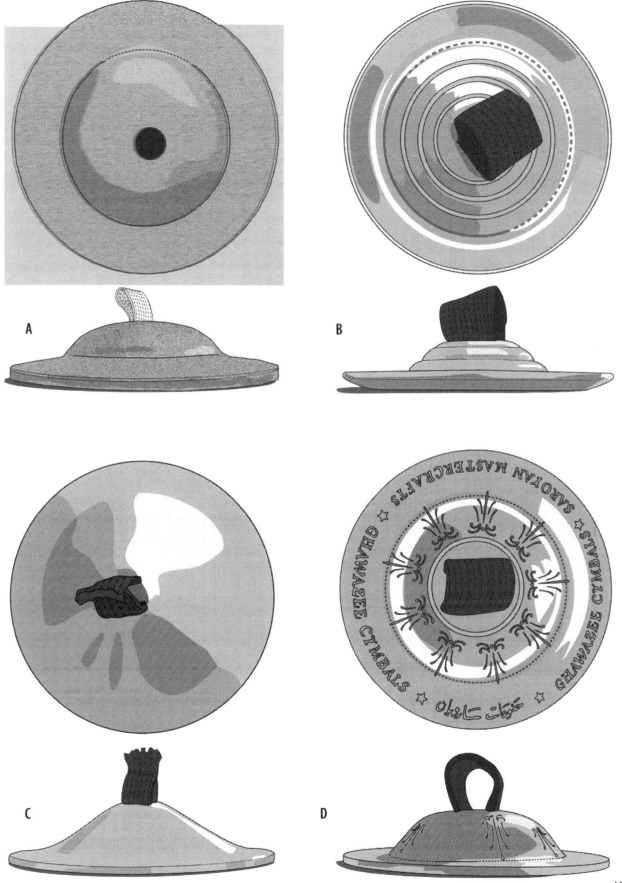

A

B

C

D

SAROTAN MASTERCRAFTS

GHAWAZEE CYMBALS

GHAWAZEE CYMBALS

صنوف كارده

Grades of Finger Cymbals

Like most things in this world, there are several different levels of quality in finger cymbals. Each style has its own set of qualities and properties, and being aware of the differences will help you get the set of instruments that's right for you.

Costume Grade - You will find many different styles of costume grade zills, and in photos these will fool you. They look like instruments, but are more like decorative jewelry worn with a costume to complete the illusion of a belly dancer. You often find this style for sale in seasonal costume shops for Halloween Gypsies, harem girls, and belly dancers. While made of metal, no effort is made by the manufacturer to give a pleasing tone when struck together. Unfortunately, costume grade zills are the most common and widely available style of zill. While you can start out playing costume grade zills to develop hand strength and finger dexterity, most people are not satisfied with the poor quality sound.

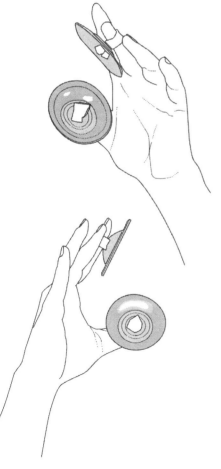

Student Grade - These are smaller, lighter weight zills made by major zill manufacturers as entry level products for class, practice, and performance. These zills will have a nice tone, but will have flatter bells, and a fainter higher ring. Smaller, lighter weight zills are an excellent place to start to build up your speed and precision. As you develop as a performer, and decide that dancing with zills is going to be part of your ongoing repertoire, you will want to graduate to the next level of finger cymbals.

Pro Grade - For public paid performances, professional dancers require zills that are loud enough to be heard in a noisy restaurant, have a beautiful tone that is pleasing to the ear, and produce a variety of clear and distinct sounds. Pro grade zills are often beautifully embellished to draw the eye of the audience. Two of the most well respected names in Middle Eastern belly dance zills today are Saroyan zills and Turquoise International.

Concert Grade - These are the largest, loudest and most expensive of all the finger cymbals. These zills can often dwarf a dancers hands, and limit the execution of complicated arm and hand movements while playing. The size and weight are designed for play in a band or orchestra environment by a musician who isn't dancing. These finger cymbals are frequently made from cast bronze. These are often made by professional instrument companies and can be quite expensive. The best known concert grade finger cymbal producers are Zildjian and Sabian.

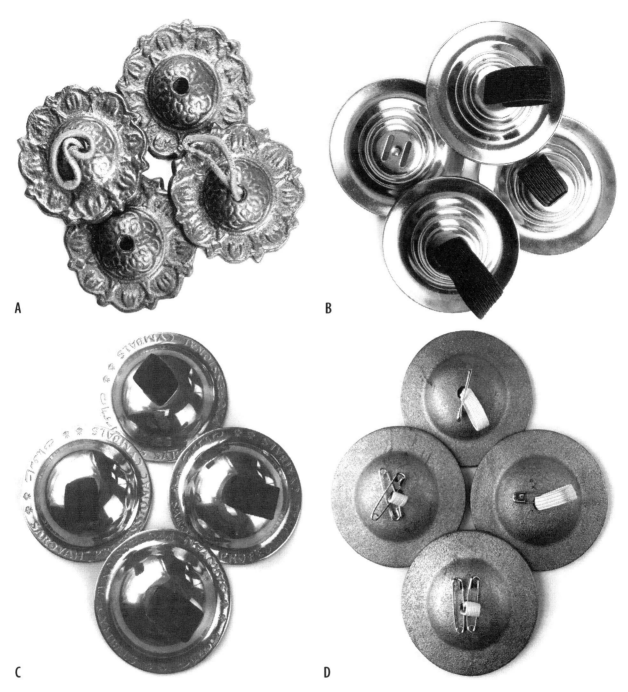

A

B

C

D

Here are examples of four of the most common grades of finger cymbals.

A - Costume grade - These cast mystery metal finger cymbals from India were purchased from a temporary Halloween shop.

B - Student grade - High quality but budget friendly option from a specialty belly dance finger cymbal maker, Saroyan Mastercrafts.

C - Profesional grade - Thicker, heavier, louder, and more dynamic zills from Saroyan Mastercrafts.

D - Concert grade finger cymbals - These cast bronze finger cymbals from Zildgian are very large and have tremendous volume and sustain.

Selection & Preparation

Now that you know a little bit more about the history of zills and how they are made, the next step is to invest in a set of finger cymbals and learn to play. But where does one start? There are many questions to consider before making an investment. No matter if this is your first set, or you are adding to a growing collection, you will have many options to choose from.

Ask yourself, what zills are right for me? Where can I buy a good set of zills? Which brands are best? What kind of tone do I like? How much do they cost? Ultimately, the best set of finger cymbals for you fits your budget, skill level, and your style. But what exactly does that mean?

Over time, most performers build a wardrobe of finger cymbals to suit a variety of performance needs. No one pair of zills will fit the needs of every single performance situation. When reaching for a set of zills, an experienced dancer will consider a variety of issues before choosing the perfect finger cymbals for that moment. Knowing what is important for you and your dance will help you select the best instruments for your collection.

The zills at left were my collection in 2005. Notice the difference in sizes and different finishes of the metal. What you cannot tell from this photograph is how they sound. Each set of zills has a completely unique voice. Today my collection is much bigger. You can see most of my zills on page 105.

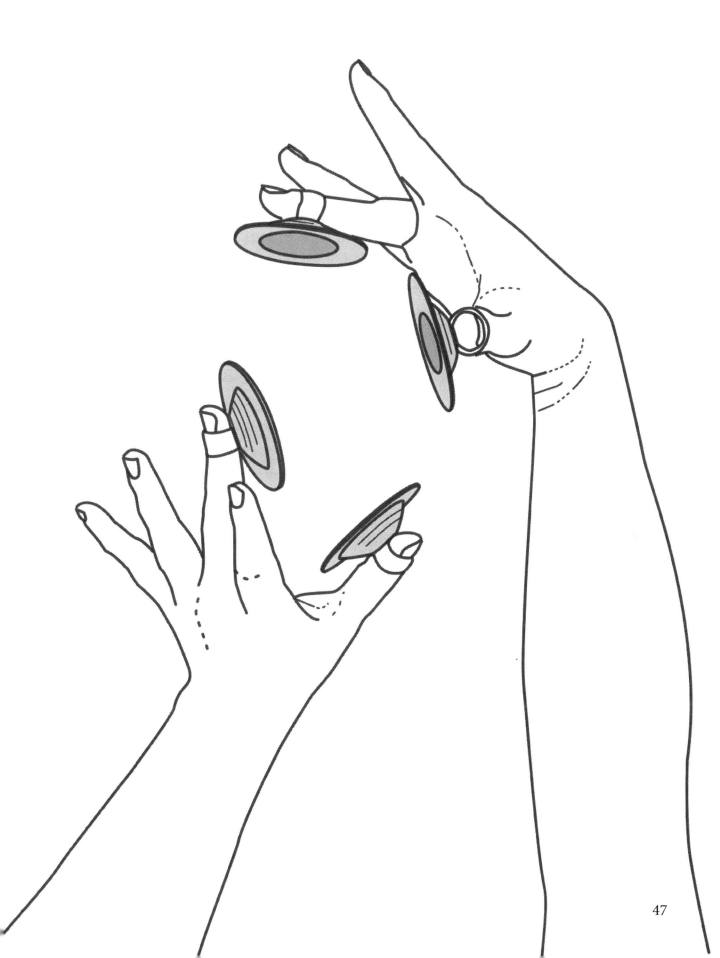

Consider your budget

Perhaps the most important factor in your purchase is your budget. If you're just starting out, you don't want to invest in large, expensive, pro-quality zills. It's easy to become discouraged with a slow learning curve if you are trying to play instruments that are too heavy. You may also decide you don't really care for playing zills so start with affordable student-grade zills.

Choose a tone you like

Every set of zills will have a different tone. Lower quality finger cymbals have shorter ring times and little sustaining ring. Cheap zills may have a thunky, flat, or slightly off-key tone. More expensive pro-quality zills are often thicker and heavier and produce a more musical, sustaining ring. Concert quality zills are often quite large and very loud. These are not designed for dance performances, and are often unwieldy to play while dancing. Some dealers put out sound files with samples of their zills being played. Of course, the best option is to buy them in person at a dance or music festival or event.

Pick a volume for your venues

In addition to the tone of your finger cymbals, consider the natural volume of the instruments. If you perform in a variety of venues, you will learn to choose a set of finger cymbals that create the volume you require. Large, loud zills are great for outdoor and large stage venues; smaller, quieter zills are better for more intimate performance spaces. Tiny zills are great for practice to gain speed, accuracy, and skill, and are great for practice in your living room, or in classes and workshops where large groups are all playing at the same time.

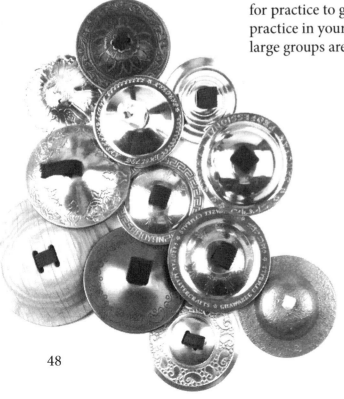

Since 2005, I've add a variety of zills to my collection. Some were choosen to bring a new sound. Some of the more unique zills I've aquired are a set of wooden zills for practicing late at night. I bought the pair at top for their dark color, but they turned out to be quite clanky. But I love the lotus pattern, and they look great sitting on my tray, and while I keep my good Saroyan zills tucked away, these lotus zills can sit out.

Selecting by Size

Many performers begin with smaller zills to build hand strength, develop basic proficiency, and gain mastery over finger cymbal playing techniques. Once you have achieved a level of success playing and dancing with smaller zills, you may find yourself ready to move up to a bigger sized set. A good rule of thumb is to start small and affordable, and work your way up in size and quality.

The right size zills for your hands are ones that you can play comfortably and use to make a variety of different sounds. Zills that are too small, like the ones at the top right, are more difficult to dampen in the crook of your thumb. If your hands are larger, but you prefer smaller zills, you will find that you might need to focus on smaller motions and precision of angle.

Large zills can be heavier, weighing down the dance movements of the hands, slowing down your speed, or affecting your tonal precision. Some instructors advocate practicing with larger, heavier finger cymbals to build strength, while other teachers prefer working with lightweight student zills to gain faster mastery and precison.

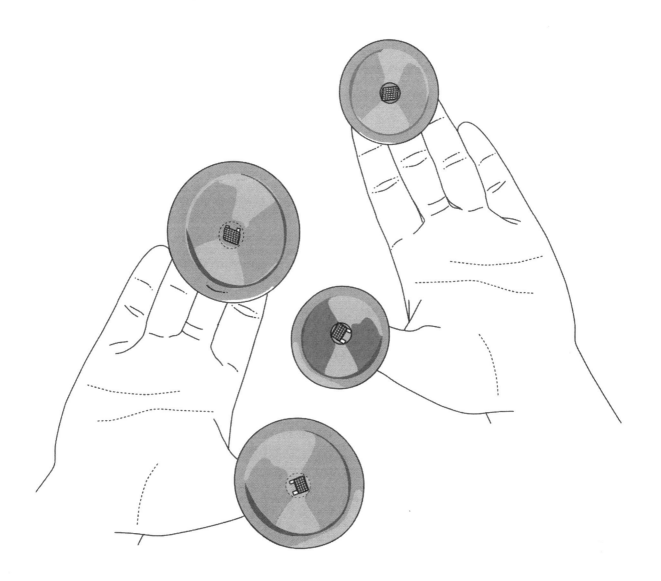

Zills vary in size from tiny zills designed for small hands like the 1.75" "MiniZills" opposite top compared to the 3" "Dervish" model on the opposite right, both from Saroyan Mastercrafts. Bigger zills are available for performers with larger hands, and musicians who are planning on performing with bands and orchestras.

Most dancers prefer zills in the 2" to 3" range for performances. In the illustration above, you can see the same pair of hands wearing a smaller 2" pair compared to larger 2.75" pair. As you become more comfortable playing with zills, you will find you can handle bigger and heavier sets.

More Zill Selection Tips

Select a metal you prefer
Many dancers collect a group of zills for different purposes, looks, and styles. One approach that many dancers take is to coordinate their zills with their ensembles, picking silver sets to go with silvery costumes, copper to coordinate with copper, and of course brass or golden hues to go with gold-toned costumes. Developing a wardrobe of different metallic hues can help you achieve a complete head-to-toe coordinated look.

Start your quest with your instructor
Most dance teachers will have a lead on places to purchase finger cymbals and recommendations for brands and styles they prefer. Some instructors, especially zill specialists, will have a number of different styles for you to try on in class and experiment with. If you are studying belly dance via distance classes, look for information on the websites and blogs of your favorite dance instructors.

Ask dancers you admire
If you see a dancer playing zills that sound good to you, ask them for the manufacturer and style of their finger cymbals. They might be playing a set that is easy to buy, and even share their source. But many dancers inherit zills from their instructors, fellow dance students, and troupe mates, so don't be discouraged if the performer you ask doesn't know the full origin story of their instrument.

Further research
When searching for zills to add to your collection, do more research to find out which finger cymbals are being talked about, reviewed, and performed with. Some cymbal companies include audio files so you can hear the tone of the zills before you purchase them. At events, be sure to touch and try as many different pairs of finger cymbals as you can. When you hear a set you like, ask the performer for the brand and model.

Preparing Cymbals

Zills are worn on the thumbs and middle fingers of both hands. The elastic, which you size to fit your specific fingers, sits at the base of your nails, positioned directly over the cuticle line. They should be very tight, tight enough, in fact, to prevent them from not only wobbling, but also from flying off during a spin. To ensure that you have them positioned correctly on your fingers, hold your hands together, in prayer pose. Your zills should touch rim to rim on both the middle and thumb.

Elastic

Although most finger cymbals initially come with black elastic, you can change it out for other colors and styles. While this is a small detail, the elastic of your zills is visible to your audience, and can pull a strange sort of focus for some types of viewers. People interested in your cymbals are the most likely to notice the details of elastic shape, style, and color. If you are going to be circulating in crowds talking about your dance, costume, and props, take an moment to consider the quality of elastic. If it looks too worn, discolored, or dirty, you may want to consider an upgrade. Here are a few things to consider when thinking about changing your finger cymbal elastic.

Many finger cymbals come with elastic that is too loose, too flimsy, or too uncomfortable. Rope elastic, like that pictured above top, can be very biting, and creates a lot of wobble.

Inexpensive elastic that is too stretchy, above lower, will continue to stretch and stretch until it no longer holds the zill to the finger.

Thick, no-roll style elastic, like the white and black below, will provide the best support and control.

- **Black elastic** – Most zills arrive from the manufacturer with black elastic. This is an excellent choice if you perform outside as black will generally show less dirt and wear and tear than white elastic.
- **White elastic** - The most widely available "color" of elastic, white elastic creates a clean modern look.
- **Match your skin tones** - Use pink, flesh or clear elastic to match the skin tone of your hands. This will make your zills appear to float on your fingers.

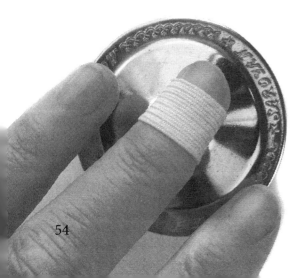

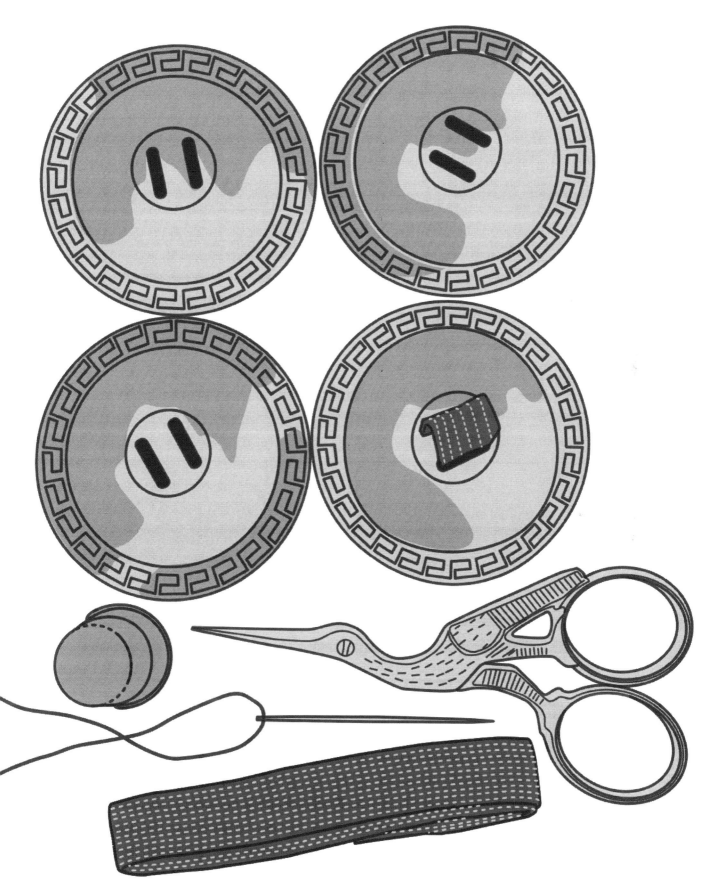

Test Your Fit

Whenever you change your elastic, make sure to do a "test dance" at home and play your full range of tones to ensure that the elastic is perfectly sized and won't fly off in a spin. Many dancers like to cut their elastic and use tiny safety pins to perfect the fit before they secure the elastic.

Secure the Elastic

There are several approaches to securing the elastics for performance. There's no one right way to fasten your elastics.

- **Safety Pins** – Zill elastic is frequently changed by performing dancers. Pins offer the ability to fine-tune the zill fit over time and allows a dancer the ability to make quick changes due to weight fluctuations. A disadvantage is that pins have been known to pop open at inopportune times or to affect the tonal quality within the bell of the zill.
- **Knots** - A traditional method, this technique works best when using round elastic versus flat elastic. Knots are secure and actually get tighter as the zills get used. However, they offer no adjustments, and can create a large lump, which can affect the tone of the cymbal.
- **Stitching** – For a permanent and secure solution that reduces bulk under the bell area, hand stitching the zill elastic is an excellent choice. However, like knotting, it becomes very difficult to make subtle fit changes. This is a good choice for a dancer who likes a very tight fit, and who doesn't experience finger swelling.

Put your zill on and give it a try before you secure it down completely. You want to position your elastic between the base of your finger nail and the first kuckle of your middle finger or thumb.

Inside of Zill - Sewn

Inside of Zill - Safety Pinned

Inside of Zill - Knotted

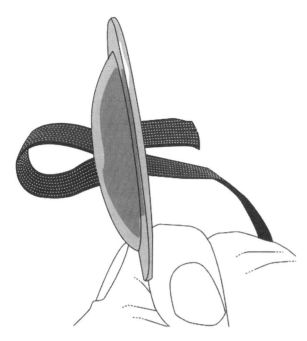

Begin by feeding the elastic through both the slots of the finger cymbal. Be sure to fit it to your thumb or finger before you cut to prevent accidentally cutting the elastic too short.

Make any fitting adjustments before cutting the elastic. Leave space to accomodate your closure preference.

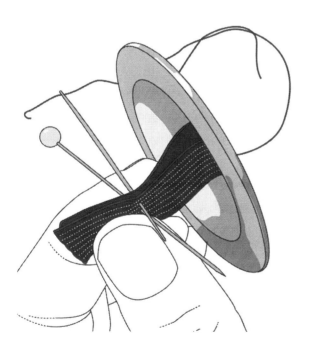

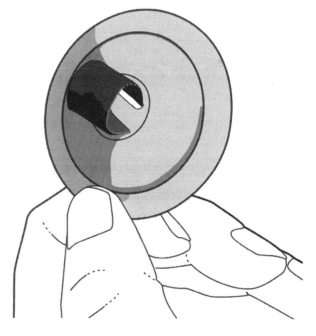

In this demo, the elastic is marked with a pen, then the elastic is pulled to the underside to stitch. You can also choose to knot or pin the elastic.

Once your elastic is secured using the your method of choice, put the whole set on and play them. If they all fit and function perfectly, you're done!

Mark your thumb zills

To make your thumb cymbals stand out from those fit to your fingers, you may want to add some small yet distinctive marking to, at a glance or touch, differentiate between finger and thumb elastic. If you are a visual person, you may want to add a dot or marking of permanent marker or even brightly colored fingernail polish to your elastic or the inside of your zill.

For dancers who want to tell their zills apart at a touch, you can add an extra tiny safety pin, double knot, or even stitch a small bead to the thumb elastic. This is of particular use if you put your zills on during a performance, and want to avoid looking down for too long at the instruments in your hand. Then, as in all things, practice putting your zills on and taking them off as part of your rehearsal of a particular choreography or dance scenario so that to ensure that you have complete mastery over the process of mounting and dismounting your zills.

Decorating your elastic

If you want your finger cymbals to go way over the top, you can embellish your elastics as if they are jewelry. Using sew-on sequins, beans, and rhinestones, you can turn a plain elatic into an embellished part of your costume.

If you have a large collection, you can transform one set of zills to coordinate with the dominant color in your wardrobe. If you perform under bright lights, sequins and rhinestones will flash with the metal and add that ultimate finishing touch when coordinating with your wardrobe. Some dancers choose not to wear rings, and an embellished elastic will give the illusion of jewelry .

The set of zills onthe right have been prepped for performace with the elastic stitched into place, emebllished with a rhinestone to catch the light through arm movements, and a bead stitched to the elastic inside the bell to identify the thumb zills by touch.

Playing Finger Cymbals

No book can teach you how to play a musical instrument. But in this section, we present you with ways of thinking about your finger cymbals and provide directions for how to put them on, their alignment, the sounds they can produce, and how they relate to the music of belly dance.

Finger cymbals are capable of producing a variety of musical sounds. Expensive, tuned zills can be exceptionally versatile, providing a host of subtly different tones produced by variations in strike force, speed, and angle. Instructors of zill playing will break down the most important tones in different ways. Thera are many different schools of thought, with some teachers focussing on as little as 3 distinct sounds or up to 10 or even more basic tones. Each instructor describes, demonstrates, and teaches his or her preferred hand positions to create the tones they need for their particular method.

If you have already been studying a particular playing method, you might find the one in this book completely different. And that is completely okay! Your mission as a dancing musician is to fill your tool box of knowledge with a wide variety of styles, methods, and approaches that you can then pick and choose to use and combine to create your own unique flavor, style, and methodology. So while some this might be totally new, other parts might seem familiar, but be presented in new or different ways.

In this method of playing zills, there are four basic tones a single pair of zills can make when struck together. These tones relate to the sounds that are made by the goblet drum, the main percussion instrument of Middle Eastern music, and, consequently, the instrument that provides the main and fill beats in most belly dance music. In addition there are two more sounds created by vibrating the zills together that add texture and variety.

Every dancer has favorite poses to strike while wearing zills. One of y personal favroite is to frame the head with the arms, but turn the palms of the hands outwards. I call the pose opposite "Antler Hands." These hand positions not only create a beautiful body line, but also allows a full range of motion for the finger cymbals.

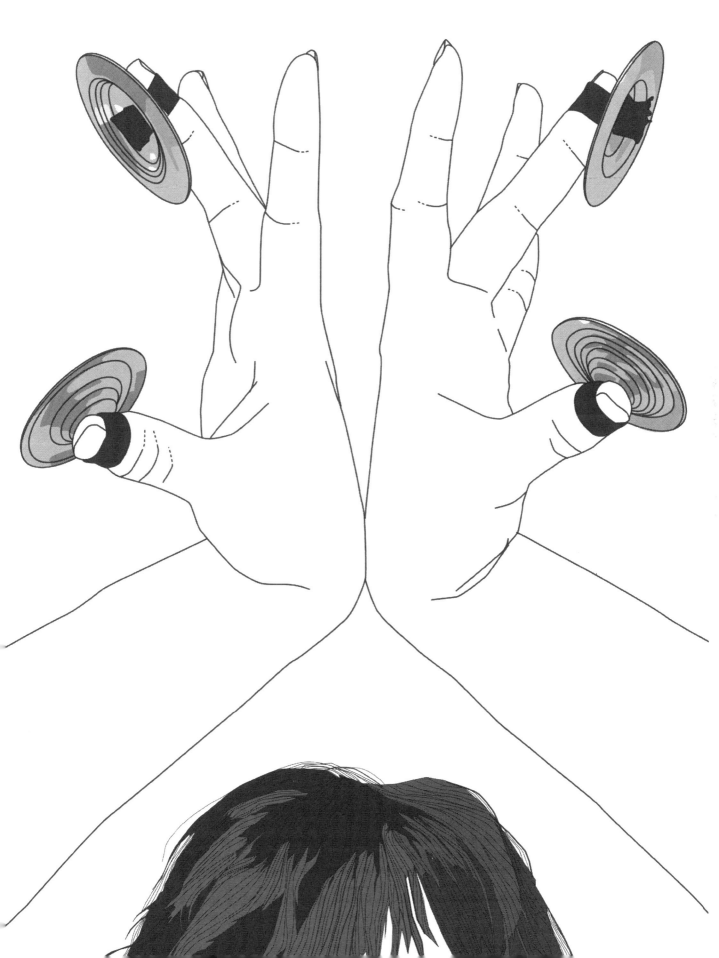

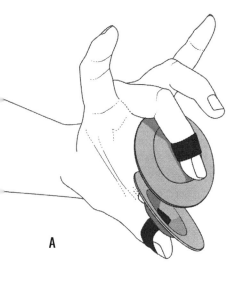

A

Creating Musical Tones

Finger cymbals can produce more than one tone. Expensive, tuned zills can be exceptionally versatile, providing the musician a host of subtly different tones. Idintifying each tone happens only through experiment and practice through modulation the hand position to create variations in strike force, speed, and angle.

Zill placement

As stated earlier in the preparation section of the book, finger cymbals are worn accross the base of the nail bed of the middle finger and the the thumb of both hands. You will want to make sure to adjust your elastic and secure your fit before attempting to play your finger cymbals. Refer to page 54 for more details. Illustration A depicts the proper placement of your finger cymbals.

Hammer and anvil

The main key to playing zills is remembering to think of your hands moving in the same manner as a hammer and anvil. In this analogy, your thumb is the anvil, and it's cymbal slides from side to side, but basically travels from side to side. The finger represents the hammer, and travels up and down to strike the thumb zill. The hammer/finger is the strike force that hits the finger cymbal on the thumb. You have far greater control over the sound when you bring your finger to your thumb.

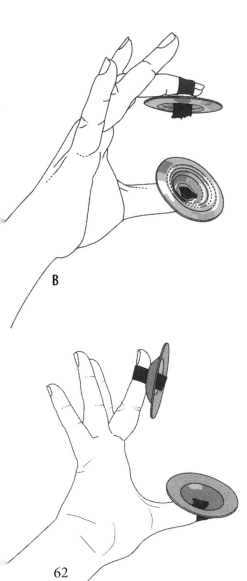

B

The finger, on the other hand, can quickly adjust it's relative position. Your goal is to keep the thumb as still as possible and strike it with your finger. You will want to practice holding your hands in a relaxed by ready position with your hand shaped like a letter C as illustrated at left in image B. Resist the urge to open your hand to wide in the shape of an L as in Position C. You will lose valuable time, and have difficulty gaining speed in your playing if you open your hands too wide.

Find your perfect neutral thumb position

When you have your zills on, the thumb can move from side to side. But there will be one spot that is ideal for playing zills. Every hand is different, so your mission is to identify that spot of perfect alignment between thumb and striking finger.

Skilled zill performers are able to quickly and accurately slide their thumb in to make more ticking, muffled sounds, to position that will strike rim to rim, creating opportunies for more bell-line ringing and longer sustains.

Thumb angle

Different dancers wear their thumb zills in different positions to control the tones they play. For many, and angled position, like that illustrated in figure B opposite, offers more opportunities for precision. While others prefer a flatter position like the illustration on this page. As you move forward in your zill playing practice, you will find your favorite thumb angles. You may, in fact, discover in time, that you prefer wearing your thumb cymbal at a specific angle to achieve a particular beat.

Flexible fingers

Your striking zill located on your middle finger will have the power to control the force of the strike. The finger can hit and bounce away to create a clear sustaining ring, or it can hit and hold to create a muted tek sound. Your finger can extend out to it's fullest to create a flatter angle of attck, allowing for a bright toned snap, or the finger can cup and hug the rim of the strike zill to hit with a softer, more muted result.

Learn your maximum capacity

Every musician has different skill, manual dexterity, speed and flexibility in their hands. Knowing what your maximum speed is, will help you choose songs to play with that won't out pace your skill. Figuring out what your maximum reach is with your middle finger will help you find out how many subtle variations of sounds you are capable of making. Hand proportion can effect your playing. Short fingered dancers might have difficulty playing long stroking brush strokes.

Each set of finger cymbals will also impact your speed and clarity. Bigger zills can be quite a challenge for people with smaller hands, while smaller zills can be challenging to muffle. This is one of the reasons why some dancers and musicians aquire sizable collections of finger cymbals.

Only through time, practice, and experimentation will you gain an understanding of your ideal hand positions. Take every opportunity you can to practice, paying attention to the feel, and observing your hand positions as you go.

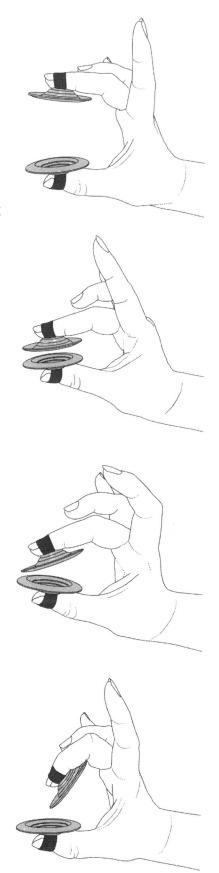

Ring

This is a clean smooth hit and bounce of two of the ringing edges or rims of the zills. The lasting ring tone is called the sustain. This sound is achieved with a quick tap of the zills slightly offset to each other.

Many highly accomplished zill players strive to achieve a nearly unending sustain with one hand while they carry heavier beats so it almost sounds like two people are playing.

Some dancers like to wear and play their zills so they hit squarely face-to-face, hitting both edges of the rim simultaneously. To maintain a long ringing sustain, a squared hit must have the edges hit simultaneously for the best quality sound. If one zill is slightly angled, it can hit a fraction of a beat slower, breaking the ring. This effect is great when used intentionally to create a sonic effect.

For dancers with single holed zills that have an inherent wobble on the fingers, speed becomes essential. The striking finger needs to hit with quickness to avoid the double strike that the wobble can create.

Each zill master has a slightly different hand position they prefer. Pay attention to the masters and really experiment until you find what works best for the architecture of your hand.

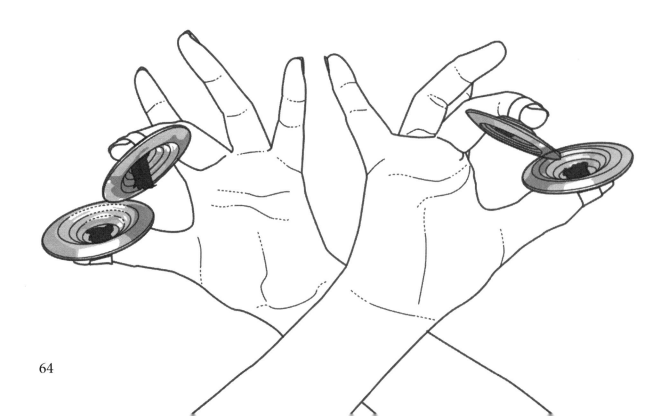

Hand alignment to make a ring:
To achieve the clearest bell-like sound with a long sustain, your finger cymbals should be offset with each other so that one rim of the striking finger hits one rim of the thumb. The stroke is a quick strike and lift, an almost bouncing motion. Above is a view from above your stroking finger, and below is a view from the thumb side.

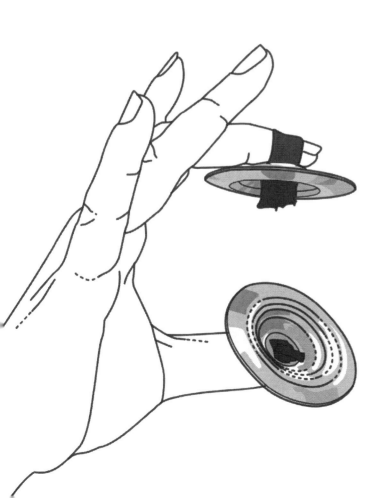

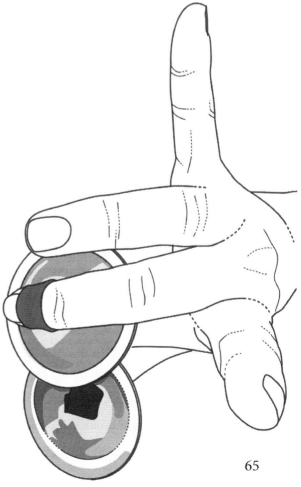

65

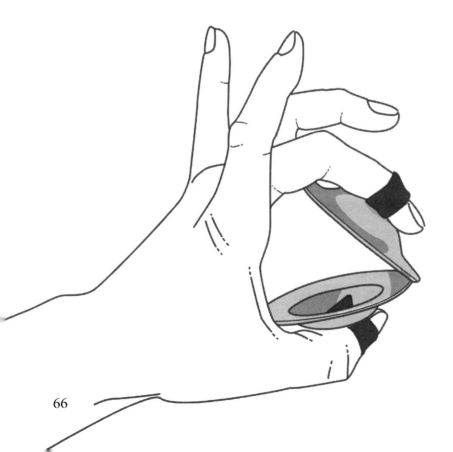

Muted Ring or Tek

This is a partial ring, where only one zill from a pair creates the sustain. Unlike a clean pure ring, with both zills ringing, the "tek" sound is partially muffled, the player controlling the amount of ring generated by .

The first way to mute a single zill is to place your ring finger, index finger, or both onto the striking zill as shown in the picture on the right. As you practice, you will discover that one finger muting and two finger muting create slightly different tones, which you can use to full advantage, especially when playing a capella and all the nuances of your instrument are audible to the audience.

The second way of muting your zills is to tuck an edge of your thumb zill into the web of your hand as illustrated bottom left. When you mute your thumb zill, you change the angle of attack on the stroke, which can lead to many more subtle variations of tone.

Some dancers like to combine the two, muting the strike zill and the thumb as illustrated bottom right. Practice both styles of muting so you can use the perfect technique for any given moment.

As you practice different hand positions, listen for the sound they create. Your mission is to have four clear and distinctly different sounds in your repertoire.

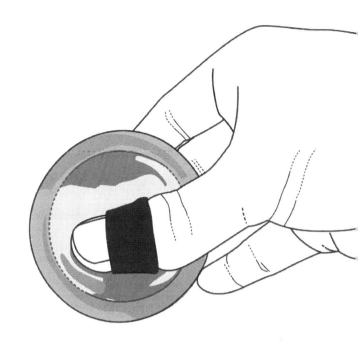

Alignment for Tek:
For a clean crisp tek sound without the ring, align the strike finger with the thumb so both zills perfectly align, the rims striking head on and holding for a moment to prevent a ring tone. Above is a view of the alignment fromt the strike finger view.

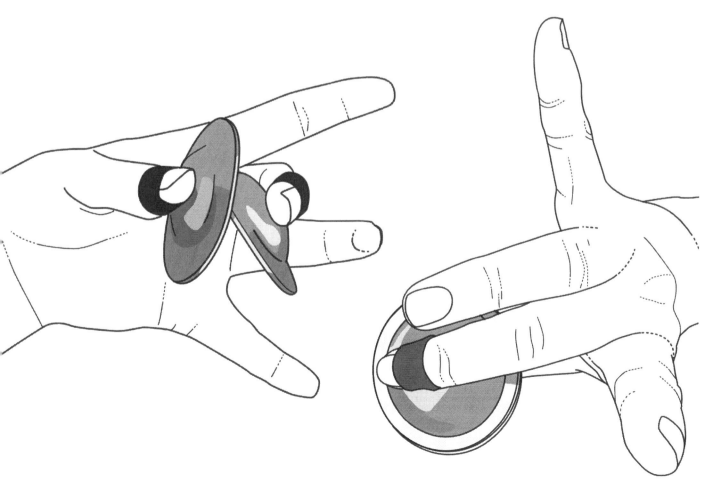

Tick or Ka

Many dancers will be happy with just mastering the two most dominant tones, the ring and the tek. But if you want to develop your skill at adding more nuances and subtleties, you will want to perfect the third sound analogous to the drum, the tek. The "Ka" sound is made by creating a T shape with your ring finger forming the top bar, and your thumb turning to make the upright.

This t-shape allows you to play several different tones. You can choose to play this tone with the striking will open and ringing like the image below left. Or you can choose to lay your fingers onto top of your striking zill to fully muffle the sound, eliminate the ringing sustain and make a sharp tek sound. The lower right image shows a fully muffled version of this hand position.

You also have the power to modulate the sound by moving your thumb so the upright is positioned is aligned with the rim, or, like the opposite image, more deeply pressed into the bell of the cymbal. Perfecting several different "Tek" sounds will allow you to create more dynamic changes in sound.

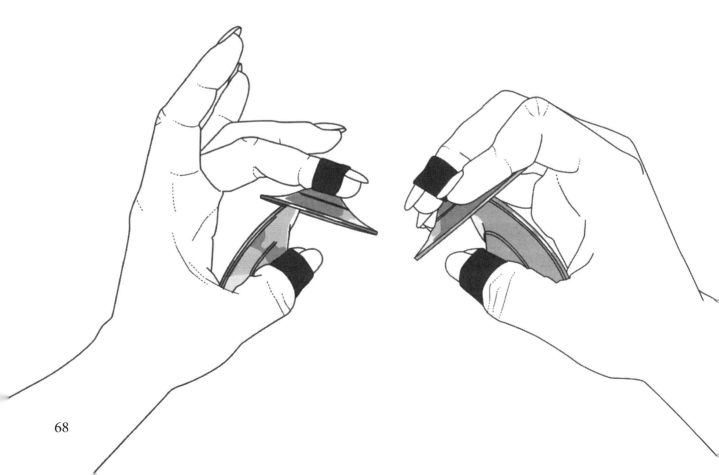

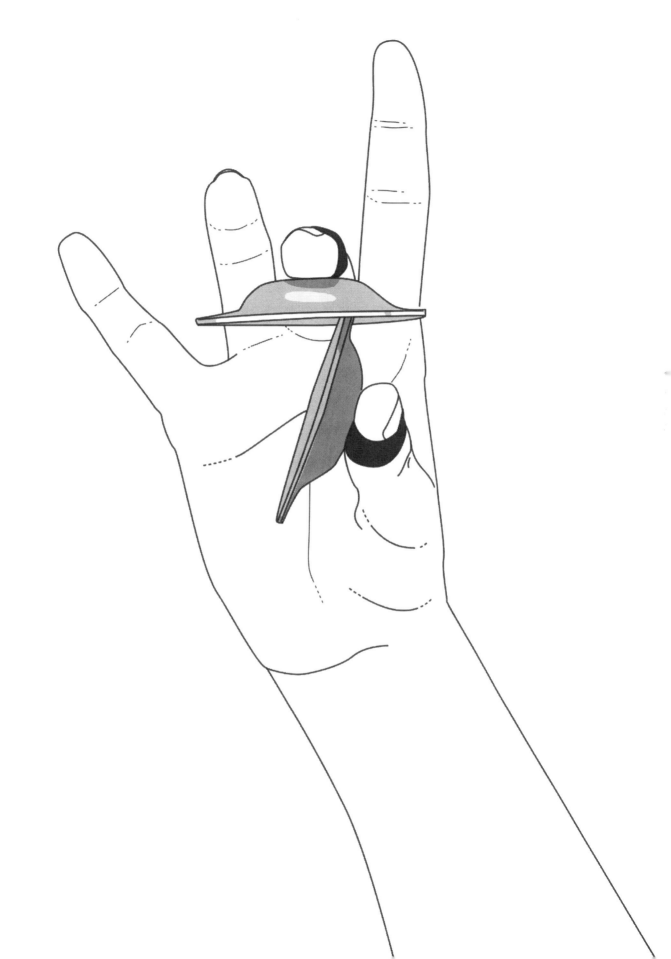

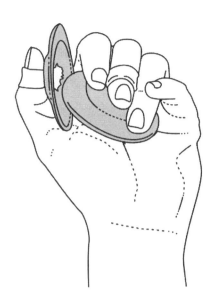

Clack or Clap

This is a zill tone that is created without a ring. The zills are cupped into the palm of the hand to eliminate the sound of the ring and create a clap or clacking noise. The cupped hands create a hollow box that helps the noise resonate, so while the hands looked muffling, the resulting tone can be quite loud.

In addition to laying your fingertips onto the striking or finger zill, the thumb zill is turned and tucked into the webbing of the hand to muffle the ring. The tighter and more tightly cupped the hand is, the softer the sound will become. If you want the muted tone, but still want it to maintain volume, practice the thumb webbing tuck, with keeping the palm exposed to alow the sound to resonate.

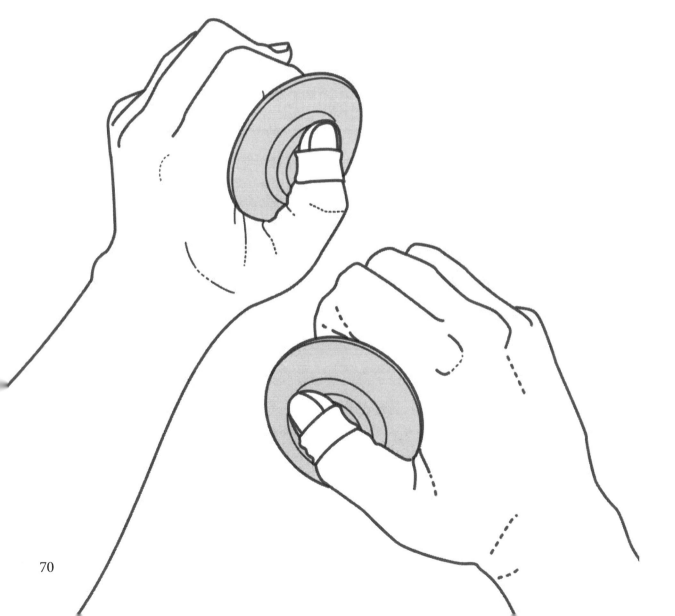

Brush

This is a unique variation where the two faces are slid against each other. Every pair of zills will create a different tone from this which adds texture and depth to traditional patterns. This sound can be very subtle, and is a great texture to add, especially when your music is soft or while adding complexity to a zill solo. Remember to keep your hand very relaxed and your zills very close together so as you swing your hands from side to side, the rims of your zills brush against each other. The hand movement is one of flipping or rolling from the wrist, and some dancers find this easiest to do when the zills are hanging down and the fingers are completely relaxed.

Every set of zills will require different angle of approach and pressure through the slide to create a sound that appeals to your ear and is useful in your musical repretoir. Just be aware that some zills won't make attractive or musical brushing tones. So if you try and can't "find" this tone in your instruments, know that it might be the finger cymbals themselves, and not your technique.

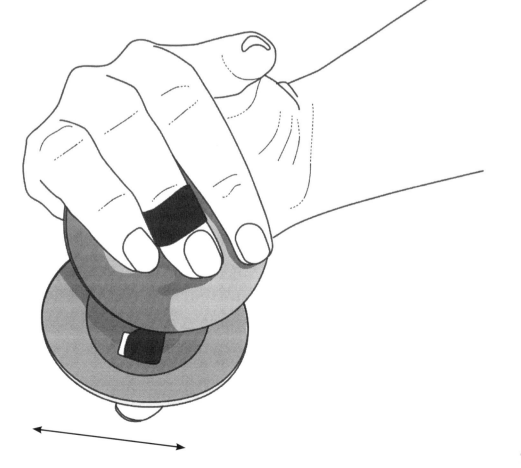

Using both hands

One of the best ways to further enhance your zill performance is with two-handed combined sounds. As a dancer, you will want the option to play all four finger cymbals accross, thumb to thumb, finger to finger, or in other combinations. All the same subtle tonal nuaunces you can achieve

Two-Handed Ring

This is the sound of all four zills hitting face-to face during a clapping of the hands. This tone is similar to the clack, but generally creates more of a ring tone. If the clap is held together, the dancer produces a flat, metallic tone.

Experiment with tapping your zills together, finger to finger. With practice, you can create all of the same sounds you can make with one hand.

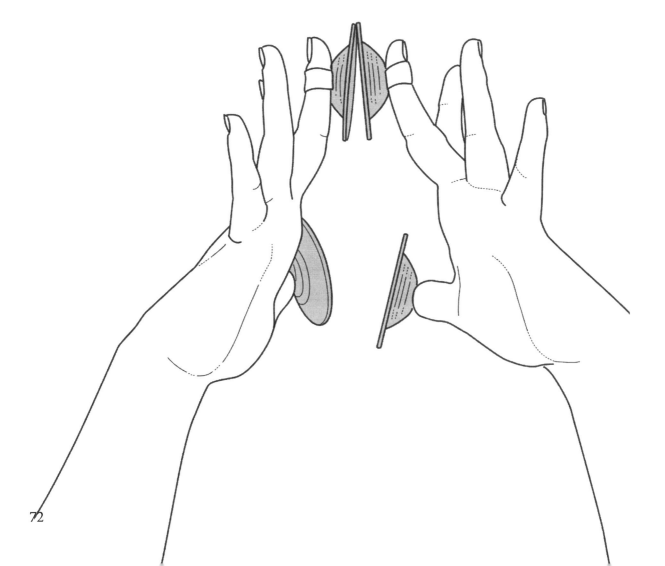

Two-Pair Clap

Clapping with all four zills makes two distinct sounds. If you clap and hold, you will get a dampened metallic tone. If you allow your zill to hit hard and bounce away, you will create a loud clear note with maxium volume and sustain from all four zills ringing

The two-pair clap is an effective way to get the audience clapping along with your performance so think of all the positions where you can effectively clap. Clap three times and a savvy audience will take the hint and clap along with you. This is especially effective when integrated into an a capella performance where your zills are a solo instrument. Invite the audience to become additional members of your percussion section with this engaging combination of action and sound.

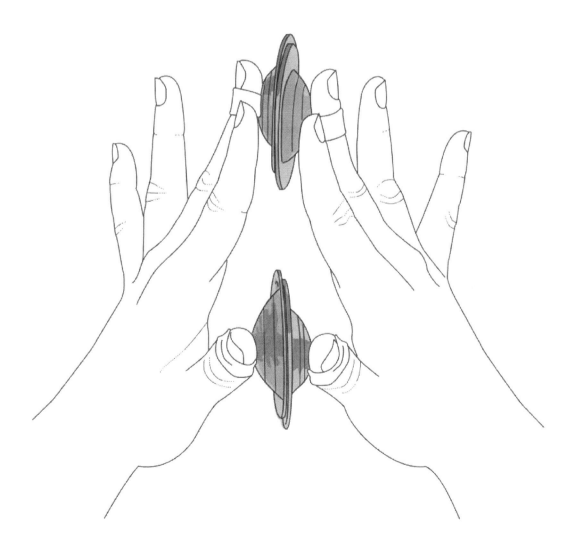

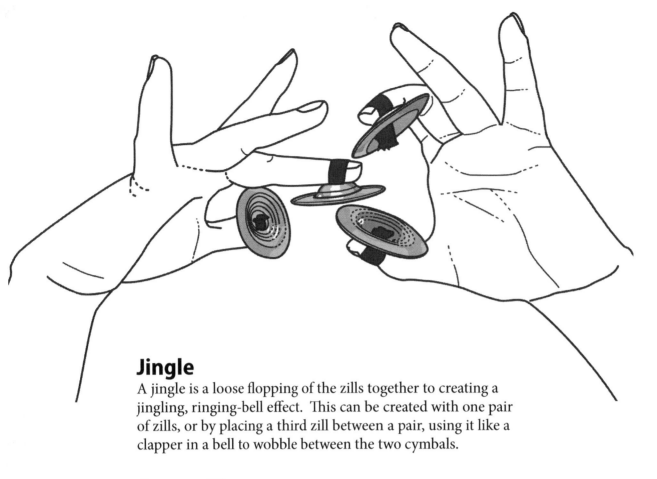

Jingle

A jingle is a loose flopping of the zills together to creating a jingling, ringing-bell effect. This can be created with one pair of zills, or by placing a third zill between a pair, using it like a clapper in a bell to wobble between the two cymbals.

Accent Ring

As you dance and move through various positions of your arms and and hands, you can create moments where your hands will interact to create clear bright ringing tones using both hands.

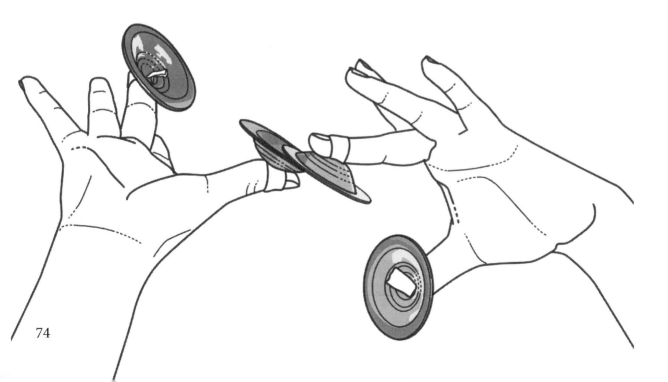

Playing Zills
Four Approaches

Once you have mastered making the different tones, stringing them together to make more complicated patterns.

Play with the drum
One approach commonly used by dancers is to echo the drum rhythm with their zill work. They can play an "open" version or a more filled in version – or even a syncopated version that accentuates the underlying drum while adding something new to the overall sound.

Play with the melody
Many dancers play with the melody line, accenting bits and pieces of the music, using set patterns of two's, three's and four's to accentuate the flow of the song. Some dancers even accentuate or echo the performer, finding dramatic places in the lyrics to accentuate.

Play on the Accents
Long pauses in your zill playing can give the audience a rest and allow you time to prepare for major zill accents. Accents can be a rapid fire triplet or quad played in time to a dramatic pop in the music or in time to a show-stopping move.

Play with your own moves
A technique used by some dancers is to use their zills to highlight their own body movements using set zill patterns to accentuate movements and motions of their dance. Developing rhythm patterns that fit particular movements or combinations will allow you the freedom to focus on your dance instead of not worrying about the exact melody.

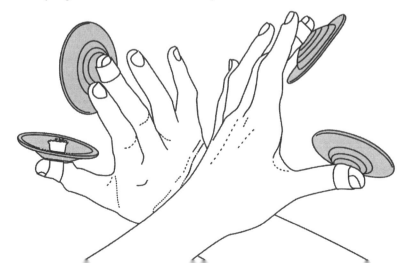

Zill Patterns

Key for pattern notations:
   R - Right Hand
   L - Left Hand
   - is a pause or rest

If you are left hand dominant, flip the L&R to fit your needs.

If you can play ambidextrously, you have the luxury of choosing which hand to feature, and can consider the needs of your choreography

One school of thought about playing finger symbals, is to use traditional patterns in a repeated, almost hypnotic drone. Having a set of simple, but effective, zill patterns in your repretoir will allow you to craft longer more complex rhythm patterns by linking different groupings together.

The patterns below, are by no means, an exhaustive list of possible zill patterns, but rather, these are the basic patterns that most dancers will pick up in their dance practice.

Numeric Based Patterns

Singles

A single ring from striking either one pair of zills, or all four zills simultaneously. A single clear bell-like tone can be used at a moment of musical emphasis, or to demarcate a change in the song or rhythm pattern. You can alter the tone of this zill strike to suit your dramatic needs and the sound of the song.

Doubles

This is two zill strikes in the place of one drumbeat. The goal is to strike with the dominant hand first, followed quickly by the second hand. Think of it like your heartbeat. You can modulate your pause to make this pattern fit most songs.

RL – RL – RL

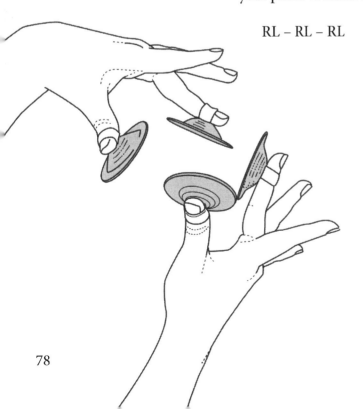

Alternating Singles

This is simply playing doubles consistently. This is a good drill to use for building up speed and dexterity. This can be used for emphasis during musical builds. Try varying the quality of the sound, moving from soft to loud, slow to fast, and tick to ring while maintaining a smooth even beat structure.

RLRLRLRLRLRLRLRLRL

Triplets

Also known as a gallop or running 3's, this is the foundation pattern for most dancers today. Be aware, that for the audience, this can become very drone-like and uncomfortable to the ear if played non-stop, so be sure to break this up with periods of rest and other zill patterns.

RLR – RLR – RLR

Quads

Experienced dancers who have mastered the triplet and have the speed and dexterity, the next step up is the quad. The goal of the quad is to hit your zills four times, in the space of three. This is a display of virtuosity that many dancers strive to achieve with their zill playing.

Combining Patterns

Once you have mastered singles, doubles, triplets and maybe even more, you can now use these patterns as building blocks to create more interesting phrases. While some dancers feel most comfortable playing a droning triplet. Most audiences prefer to have the zill playing broken up by changes in pattern.

In time, many dancers develop signature phrases from these building blocks. One example that is popular at moment in the region I live is to finish off a series of triples with a pause and then three slow rings.

RLR - RLR - RLR - RLR - RLR - Ring - Ring - Ring

The possibilities are nearly endless. Listen to a lot of music and practice fitting your pattern blocks into songs. Some dancers like to create "Zill-og-raphy," finger cymbal notations that go with a particular song or set.

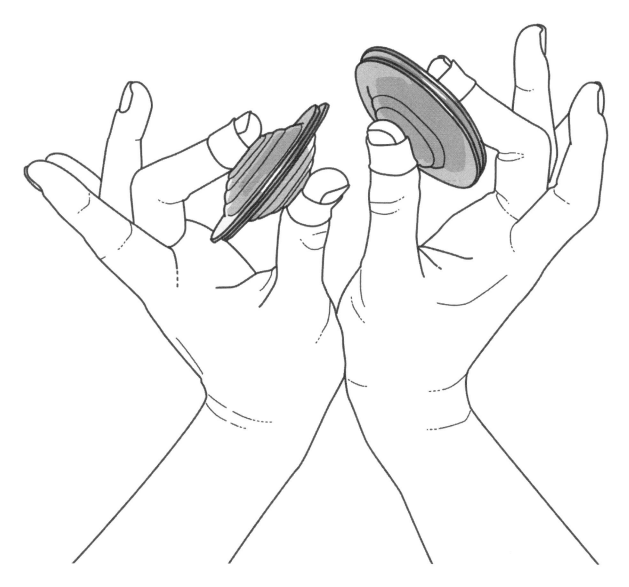

Syncopated Beats

There is a fine art to syncopation, or playing zill in opposition to your music. This happens when you stress one of the softer beats or break the meter of the music with a tone that doesn't match on existing beat.

Insert extra beats

One approach to syncopating is to insert extra beats. Think of it like this, everywhere you can play three beats, or a triplet – you can also play a very quick four.

Clap on the rests

Another approach is to clap in the pauses or rests in the music. This method relies on your timing and taste to either hit and let your zills ring, or, like the image above, to hit and hold to create a more percussive, less bell-like effect.

Common Drum Rhythms

Earlier we mentioned that zills have tones that can be played like sonic analog to the sounds made by a dumbek. In this section, we present the most popular drum rhythms broken down with two suggested playing methods.

Reading drum notation

Below is one of the most common form of drum notation. if you search for Middle Eastern drum pattern charts, you will find many variations on this theme. To make these charts useful for dancers, we've selected the most simplified versions of each rhythm. Here's the key to reading these charts:

First line - Name of the Rhythm and it's Time Signature
Second Line - Counting line to divide the meter
Third Line - The Drum notation of the most basic beats
    Dum - deep voice (dominant hand)
    Tek - high tone (non-dominant hand)
    A or Ka - high tone (dominant hand)
Fourth Line - Simple zill notation
    B - Both Zills struck together
    R - Right
    L - Left

When playing your drum patterns, be consistent within your own playing skill. If you choose to play with drum analogous tones, follow the drum pattern line. If you want to simplify your playing and use just one ringing tone, play the second line, striking with both hands to get more volume to accent the dum's and playing single strikes of L(eft) and R(ight) for quieter teks and kas. Both of these strategies can be used together during a single piece to highlight different parts of the book.

Beladi (4/4) (Little Maqsoum)
1 e & a	2 e & a	3 e & a	4 e & a
Dum-Dum	Tek-a-Tek	Dum	Tek-a-Tek
B B	RLR	B	RLR

Maqsoum (4/4)
1 e & a	2 e & a	3 e & a	4 e & a
Dum Tek	tek	Dum	Tek ka
B R	L	B	RL

Saidi (4/4)
1 e & a	2 e & a	3 e & a	4 e & a
Dum Tek		Dum-Dum	Tek-a-tek
B R		B - B	RLR

Zeffa (4/4 or 8/4)
1 e & a	2 e & a	3 e & a	4 e & a
Dum tek-a-tek		Dum Tek-ka	
B R L R		B	R L

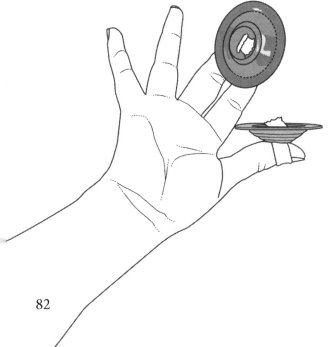

The tambourine or riq is another common percussion instrument that is often played as both lead and fill. Many dancers enjoy jingling their zills along with a tinkling riq shake to emphasize this percussion accent.

2/4 Rhythms

These rhythms are often the building blocks of classical Arabic and modern belly dance music. Often drummers will layer these basic patterns during drum solos to add texture and variety.

Ayub (2/4)
1	e	&	a	2	e	&	a
Dum			ka	Dum		tek	
B			R	B		R	

Lef (2/4)
1	e	&	a	2	e	&	a
Dum				Tek	-	a -	Tek
B				R	-	L -	R

Fellahi (2/4)
1	e	&	a	2	e	&	a
Dum	ka			Dum	ka		
B	- R			B	- L		

Malfoof (2/4)
1	e	&	a	2	e	&	a
Dum	ka	tek		ka	tek		
B	R	- L		R	- L		

8/4 Rhythms

These percussion patterns are longer and fuller, creating lots of opportunity to fill. Just be sure to always return to the dominant to maintain the clarity of the pattern.

Chiftetelli (8/4) ALWAYS pause for the full 8 in this long slow
1	e	&	a	2	e	&	a	3	e	&	a	4	e	&	a	5	e	&	a	6	e	&	a	7	e	&	a	8	e	&	a
Dum	Tek-tek			Tek-tek												Dum				Dum				Tek							
B	RL			RL												B				B				R							

Masmoudi (8/4) (two dum version)
1	e	&	a	2	e	&	a	3	e	&	a	4	e	&	a	5	e	&	a	6	e	&	a	7	e	&	a	8	e	&	a
Dum				Dum				Tek-	a-			Tek-				Dum				tek-a-tek				tek-a- tek							
B				B				R	L			R				B				R L R				R L R							

Masmoudi (8/4) (three dum version)
1	e	&	a	2	e	&	a	3	e	&	a	4	e	&	a	5	e	&	a	6	e	&	a	7	e	&	a	8	e	&	a
Dum				Dum				Dum	ka			Tek				Dum				Teck				Tek	ka			Tek	Ka		
B				B				B	R			L				B				R				R	L			R	L		

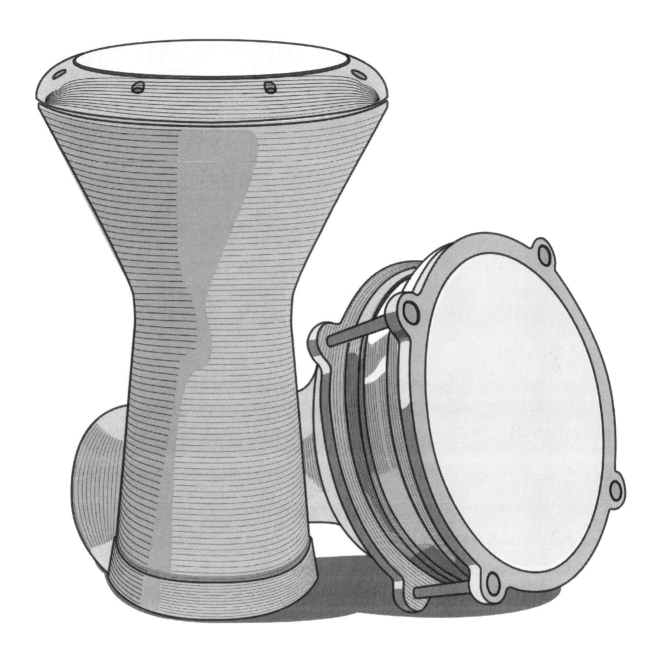

When you find music that inspires you to perform, take some time to really listen for the vairous different drum and percussion sounds. The primary drum used for Middle Eastern, North African, and Central Asian is a goblet shaped hand drum. They are called a variety of names depending on where they are made. Often there are two or three, with a lead drum playing more compli-cated riffs and other drums carrying the basic beat. Above left is an Alexandria style Egyptian doumbek. On the right is a classic Turkish style darabuka.

Beyond Basic Drum Rhythms

There are hundreds of very danceable rhythms in both classic and popular music available from the cultures of the Mediterranean, across North Africa, and the Middle East. A full compendium of drum patterns used for belly dance is outside the scope of this book. We encourage you to use our basic rhythms to build skill, strength, and endurance. Once you feel confident performing to belly dance standard patterns, use the music that inspires you and challenge yourself to move beyond the basics.

What is in a name?
This may seem a little backwards, but you really don't need to know the "name" of a rhythm in order to spot it in a song, and teach yourself to play it. While it's good to be as well informed as possible, if you have a song that inspires you to dance, don't feel limited by naming conventions. Take the songs you love, and just go for it.

Analyze
Analyze the rhythms by listening to the music over and over. As you listen to the music repeatedly, you will absorb the beat and all of the subtle nuances. With more listenings, you hear the different instruments. Listen for the structure of the music.

Diagram the Pattern
Like the patterns we presented on the previous two pages, use the drum notation of dum's and teks or your favorite zill notation system to break down the . If you can write it down, you can learn to play it. learn it, practice it, and play it.

Learn
Once you have your rough pattern notated, you can research the name by comparing it to more comprehensive drum rhythm lists in books, websites, and in videos. While knowing the name of a pattern isn't essential to play it, you may want to look it up and notate it in your dance or music journal.

Practice
When you love a piece of music and plan on performing a dance to it, begin practice on it. It's a truism that practice makes perfect. So moving through your current favorite dance pieces, and new inspiring songs while playing zills will help you prepare you body, reinforce your zill skills, and improve your hand, body, mind coordination.

Dancing with Zills

Playing finger cymbals while dancing can be terribly daunting to the new performer. Everyone has the moment where they have to just be brave and get out there and play and dance. In this next section, we cover a variety of approaches that are used to integrate zills effectively into your next performance.

Practice Practice Practice

It takes consistent, regular practice sessions to get really good at any musical instrument. With zills, you are marrying the skill of dance with the skill of playing an instrument so you need to practice both, together. It goes without saying, that you should always practise your zill playing while moving.

Practice builds strength in your arms to allow you to live your hands high over head, or completely outstretched with your zills on your fingertips. Even the smallest zills will add weight to your hands, and only through rigorous practice will you develop the muscle stretngth in your arms, neck, shoulders, and back to play for extended periods of time.

Always Practice while Moving

Unless you perform exclusively with a band, always practice when moving. Your goal is to create a strong mind and body connection, with your zills playing automatically, and with the appearance of grace and total control of every nuanced movement.

Take a moment at the beginning of each practice session to pick a topic, say "Slow beladi" or to pick a movement or combo, say "Body undulations with arm circles" so that you can target specific areas for skill building.

Create a finger cymbal practice playlist

One of the most helpful things that some teachers do is construct playlists for their students. They will select cuts with the right tempo and drum pattern so students can practice their patterns. But you don't need an instructor to do this for you. Create your own playlist featuring your favorite songs slected for the right tempo for your personal level of skill and development

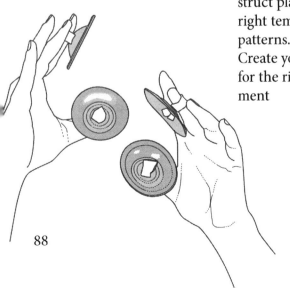

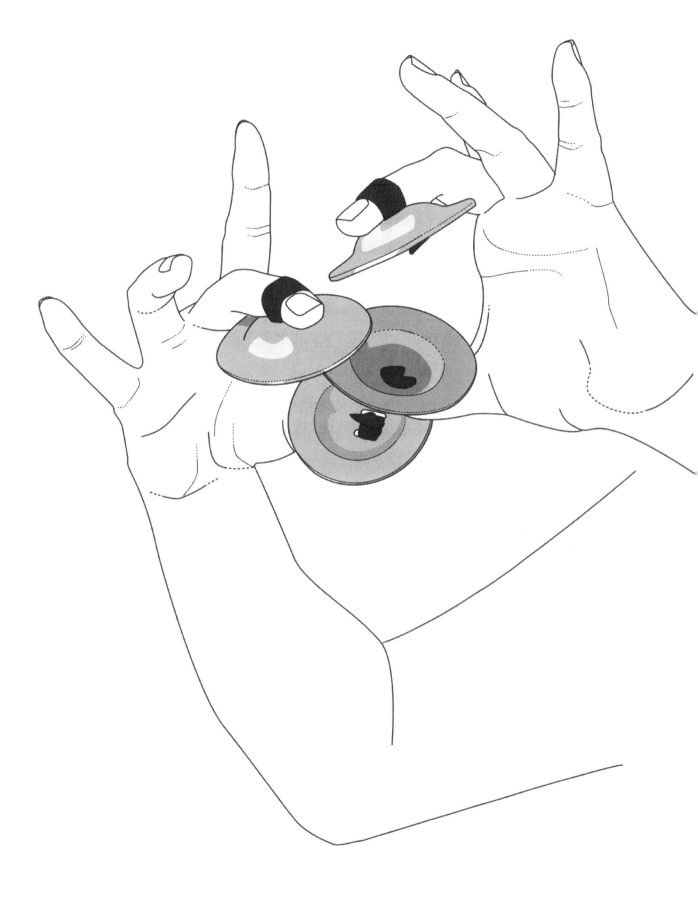

Practice Strategies

Take a zill walk

When you are first beginning, your feet serve as a natural metronome to help you maintain the beat and feel in your body when your timing is drifting off. Zilling in time with your footsteps connects your zill playing to your body in a most primal and fundamental way.

With your practice playlist loaded onto your favorite portable music listening device, it's easy to take your finger cymbals for walks with you, listening to your music and walking in time to the beat and playing your zills in time. Parks, beaches, forests, hiking trails and just walks around your own neighborhood are great times to practice with your zills.

Use a zill drill

Much like a warm up before classes, zill drills help you really cement the mind-body connection through repeated practice. Your zill drill can come from an established finger cymbal master in the form of a digital video recording that you can practice with at home. DVD's and on-line video recources offer plenty of options.

Build zill drill choreographies

If you don't want to use a pre-packed zill drill, make your own. These little practice dances are a lot like making study flash cards. No one ever needs to see your notes! Be sure when you are creating your drill choreos that you include different arm positions that you like to use in your dance. This helps not only build grace to and through those positions, but also helps you develop the strength in your arms.

Make your own practice videos

With today's technology, it's esier than ever to make video recordings and replay them easily and often. Once you have a zill drill you love and want to repeat to build mastery, informally record yourself working through it. You might want to start with you favorite warm-up before diving into your drills. And remember, while you don't have to dance, you should always keep moving and using your arms in different positions and attitudes. So make sure to include your signature poses, combinations and moves in these practice drills.

If you have recently studied with a zill master by taking a workshop at an event, take a moment immediately following the class to video record what you learned while it's fresh. Tell your future self what skills, technique, movement vocabulary and other details you learned. Make sure to perform any drills or choreography you picked up for future reference.

Muting Your finger Cymbals

Carving out practice time is vital for building skill, speed, and stamina. In our hectic world time is just one factor, the other is noise. While it might be ideal to work through your drills at 10 pm or 6 am, your family and neighbors might not be as enthusiastic. The solution? Practice with muffled zills.

There are many approaches to muffling your zills. Here are a few of our favorites:

Buy a "practice pair" and tape the rim
Using surgical tape that can easily be removed on the edges of your zills to mute the ring and sustain. If you need to use your zills, be prepared to clean any residual glue with alcohol.

Slip a draw-string bag over your zills
Many dancers repurpose small drawstring bags like the ones that jewelry sometimes come in to take down the noise. Baby mittens, like those in the middle left image, are practically perfect and readily available. Take your zills shopping with you to try them on.

Make your own custom mutes
If you are crafty, you can make a set of custom zill cozies either by making custom fit drawstring bags, round elastic covers, or using crochet like the zill mute top left.

Buy a practice pair of unconventional materials
New technology has brought a new concept, plastic practice zills made using 3D printing. Wooden zills, which can be a bit noisier, are still much quieter than metal zills. Large plastic buttons can also be turned into practice finger cymbals by stitching to elastic loops.

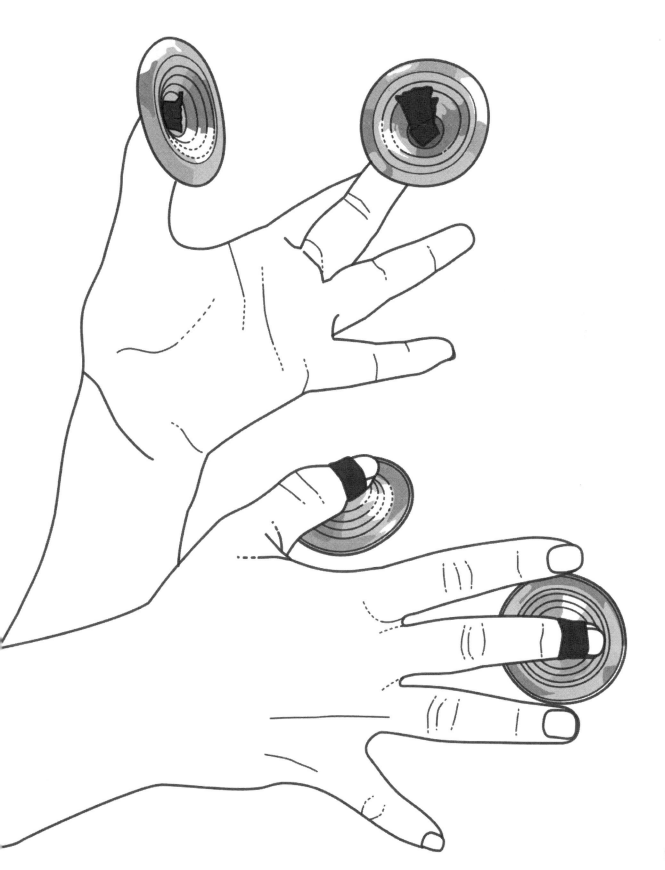

Performance Strategies

Once you have selected, purchased, and fit your finger cymbals, it's time to dance with your zills! There is no possible way a book on zills can teach you to either play or dance with zills, so in this section I'm going to share with you my top tips, strategies, and approaches to think about when practicing or planning your next performance.

Wear your finger cymbals

Even if you are a rank beginnner, put your zills on and wear them in perormance. You may not do more than the occasional accent ring, but that is okay. Your mission is to get out there and perform with them on. With time, you will be able to add patterns, complexity, and duration. Be brave, dance with your zills on.

Vary the rhythm

Even the most perfectly played triplets can get on the nerves of an audience. Don't try their patience, and instead, mix it up. Throw in accents, alternate patterns and dramatic pauses to break up the tones. Play your zills in a musical manner that mixes it up and keeps the audience excited and interested.

Accent the music

When performing to pre-recorded music, you have the luxury of knowing exactly what is coming. Prepare ahead of your performance with a series of planned accents to the music. Does the music have a dramatic pause? An exciting buildup? One approach is to anticipate these moments, and plan a strategy for accentuating them with your zills. Another is to choreograph your piece, working in your finger cymbal patterns as part of your choreography so you don't forget or waste an opportunity to showcase your skill.

Avoid drowning out the music

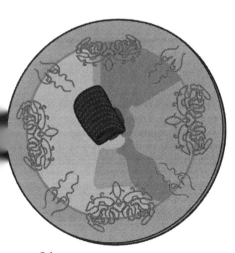

Regardless of your performing plans, listen to the music and adjust the volume so you don't drown it out. If your music is playing softly, adjust your zills by laying your fingers on the edge or cupped hands. This will reduce the ringing quality without sacrificing your zill playing completely. When mixing your recordings, make sure they the sound balance is loud enough so you don't drown out the sound.

More Peformance Strategies

Accent your dance
Many experienced dancers use sounds of their finger cymbals to accent particular combinations or movement phrases throughout their performance. One popular example is to use a jingling tone of the zills while shimmying. Another is to hit a loud ring with stacatto movements or precision isolations.

Dramatic Pauses
An effective way to accent your dance is to make a dramatic pause in your zill playing during an amazing pose, or complicated step combination. So to, playing your zills in a blazing ring while staying absolutely still has a very different, yet equally powerful energy and both of these dramatic pauses will add variety to your zill work.

Pause for Live Drum Solos
If you are performing with a band, it's important to understand the goals of the musicians you are dancing with. There may be drummer who really enjoys collaborations with a dancer, and other who are just there to support the other members of the band. It's polite to always allow a drummer to own the drum solo, by keeping your zills quiet for most of the performance and bringing them in as accent dings, or jingles that don't diminish their solo time. If you've never performed with a drummer before, it is a nice gesture to ask them if they mind if you play your zills. If they say yes, add them only to the last quarter of their performance so they have the time to shine.

Interact with a drummer in a "call and repeat"
Some dancers perform with the same band or drummer frequently, and the drum solo may evolve into more interactive format. If your drummer is encouraging you to play zills, why not try a call and repeat format. Many drum solos are structured so a drummer repeats a phrase two, four, or eight times. You can play with them by listening to their "call" and then playing a "repeat" For instance, if they play a beladi pattern, you play a beladi pattern with them, then they play alone, then you both play together. Talk to your drummer to see if this is something worth trying. This duet forges a strong dancer-musician connection that can be very entertaining to the audience.

Accent Dramatic Poses:
Some dance poses emphasize the zills and create moments within the flow of the dance where the playing of the instruments takes over and becomes the key element in the moment. Imagine dipping into a backband incrementally and hitting a loud ring or clap at each level.

Compose a zill solo

One of the most potent way for a dancer to demonstrate their virtuosity with finger cymbals is to create an a cappella performance. The zill solo can serve as a transition between parts of a larger routine or it can be structured to replace a drum solo. The longer your piece, the more time you will have to demonstrate your fullest range of subtly nuanced sounds. Here are some ideas to consider for integrating a zill solo into your performance.

The fiery entry

If you are working with live music, you can arrange with a band to enter the performance space before they begin their set. You can take a minute or two to showcase your zills, get the audience clapping and then cue the band to join you for the rest of your performance. If you are performing to pre-recorded music, tell your sound person you will be entering the stage before the music begins, and that you will be cuing them when to start. Make sure the cue is both an obvious gesture, and visible from the stage so they will not accidentally miss the start of your performance.

Build bridges

If you use pre-recorded music, you can arrange your pieces with strategic gaps between cuts to fill with artfully played zills. You can transition between up beat music to a taxim by slowing down the energy with more mellow playing, or, vice versa, you can bridge between a slow portion of your performance and an upbeat drum solo and get the audience really energized with your zill playing skills.

Replace the drum solo

When you feel you are ready, and can fill a 2 - 3 minute time slot, you can replace the drum solo with your own zill solo. If you are planning on going this route, consider creating a choreography that unifies your movement and finger cymbals. Writing down your zill patterns and the moves that go along with them will help you master both musical and dance pieces.

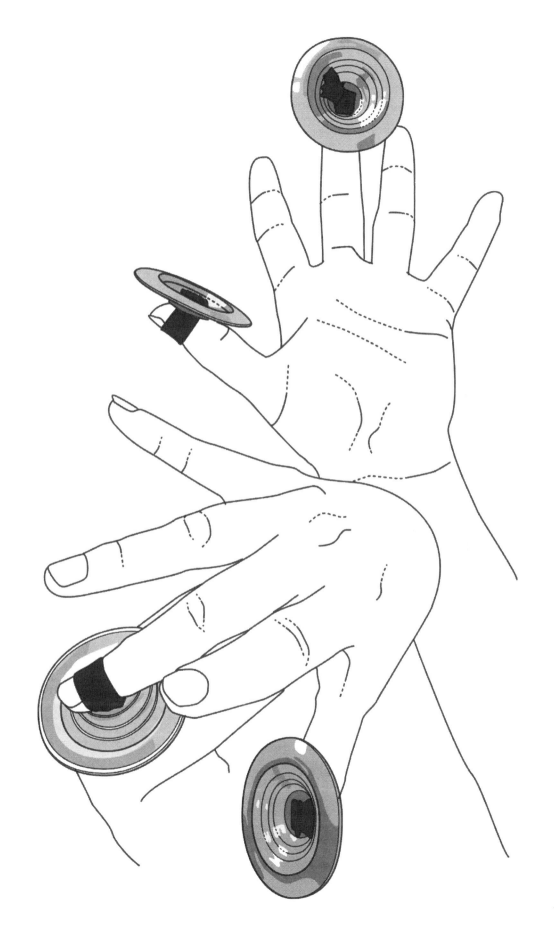

Five Part Routine

Zills hold an important role in the classic American cabaret five part set. This is a well established program that belly dancers have been using for more than century, and includes five well established parts. The use of zills, the music, and choice of props helps delineate each of the five sections. Here's a rundown of this structure, and where zills fit into the show.

Opening
This is a high energy number that gets the audience excited about the dance. Explosive and upbeat zills grabs the attention of the viewers and announces that the show is on. This is especially important in restaurants where the dancer may not have an introduction and the patrons are facing inwards to their tables.

Taxim
This portion of the music is usually slow and melodic. Taxim roughly translates to "Solo" but within the context of belly dance has come to indicate a portion of the music without drums. Most dancers will either remove their zills, or will will dance with them silently.

Prop
During this phase, a prop is introduced into the performance. This section is often flip-flopped with the taxim portion depending on the taste and style of the performer. Many dancers who perform with veil, will move the prop to right after the opening. Depending on the prop, a dancer might choose to integrate her zill playing depending on her mood.

Drum Solo
The drum solo portion is one of the hallmarks of the belly dance performance where subtle and sharp articulations of the body are timed to match or counterpose the beats of the drum. True zill masters will often compose an a' cappella zill solo to demonstrate their virtuosity.

Upbeat Close
During the close, a pro will play their zills, again. She might go into the audience to collect tips, or to pull audience members up to dance with her. It's the last impression the dancer gets to make, and it's always a great opportunity to showcase her most potent skills.

Planning for Problems

While practicing your technique, choreography, and drilling for skill building, it's also good to practice your strategies for dealing with problems. Here are some of the most common problems and techniques for planning how to cope with difficulties.

Learn to hear when you're off

Pay attention to the music and to your playing. Even the best dancers will periodically slip off of their timing and lose their place in the music. Train yourself to be aware and stop to pause occasionally. If you get off of your music, stop playing for a few measures, giving your audience a break from the sound, and you time to recompose before you begin playing again. If you have pauses built into your playing technique, it will seem natural for you to stop, and not a mistake.

Dropping a Zill

At some point in your performance career, you will find yourself losing a zill. Perhaps the elastic gave way, a thread broke, you performed a spin or you simply lost control in the heat and passion of performing. It happens to everyone at some point! Your options are to abandon the remaining zills and continue the dance without them. If this is the case, practice a zill dismount to remove and safely set your zills down without breaking the flow of your dance. Alternately, you can master a "dip" to scoop up the missing instrument. Develop your own signature "dip and remount" combination to be prepared.

Loss and Theft

If you take your zills off during your performances, be sure you place your zills in a safe zone. Before your show, scout out a location to set your finger cymbals where they will be safe. When dancing in a restaurant setting, resist the urge to set your zills on a random strangers table. You never know when they will consider this a "gift" and take them when they leave.

Using the Power Ding

One of the traditional methods for dealing with problematic customers in a professional manner is to use your zills to separate yourself from an audience member. A well placed ding near the ear can be a poignant reminder that dancers are powerful and in control.

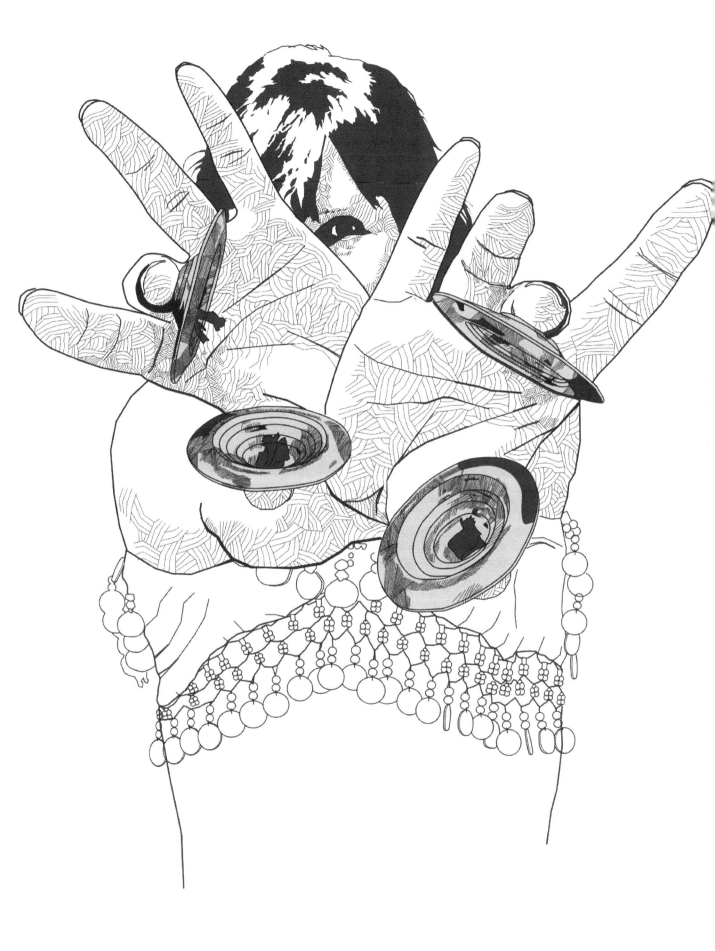

Care and Storage

Good quality finger cymbals are an investment, and it's well worth the effort it takes to safely care and store them, keeping them in good condition so they will provide you with years of excellent service. Good care will keep them bright, shiny and ringing true through many years of dance performances.

Many belly dancers consider their zills to be an essential and genre defining element of the dance. Professional dancers use their zills to simultaneously draw the attention of the the audience while demonstrating a level of virtuosity that separates them from amateur performers.

Professional and concert grade finger cymbals are quite expensive. But most of their care requires more thought and care than a high price tag. In this section, we will discuss some of the most common methods for protecting the finish of your zills. In addition, we will show you some of our favorite ways of storing and transporting zills.

Avoid chipped zills like those above by purchasing better quality zills, like this set at right from Saroyan. Better quality zills are made from solid brass, bronze, and German silver alloys, rather than a thin plated coating that can chip and flake during storage, transportation, or from simply playing them.

Care of Zills

Now that you own a set of zills and are performing with them. It's important to consider the maintenance of your instruments. A good pair of finger cymbals will last a lifetime if you invest some time caring for them.

To Clean or Not to Clean

Depending on your style, you may or may not want to keep your zills sparkling clean. There are performers who like to have a dazzling shine on their zills, using them to catch the viewer's eye and sparkle from stage. Other dancers prefer a mellower glow, allowing their finger cymbals to develop a patina on the surface. As long as the zills fit properly against the finger, and are debris free, then they should provide the same quality sound.

Shiny Zills

For shiny zills, there are several processes you can use to achieve an almost mirror finish. First clean your zills with a slightly abrasive cleanser, such as a powder kitchen cleaner to really remove any build-up on the surface. You can also use a metal cleaner specifically designed to clean brass. One all-natural cleaning solution is to wipe with pure lemon juice, or even give them a lemon juice bath, which will give them a clean glow. When the zills are clean, you can use car wax to buff the metal to your desired degree of shine.

Replacing Your Elastic

While good quality zills can provide years of service, the elastic will eventually begin to show signs of wear. Changing your finger cymbal elastic should be regular part of the routine maintenance of your performance gear. Periodically, take a moment to examine your zills. Professional dancers replace the elastic before an accident happens during performance. so look for signs of wear. Change it when it begins to loose, begin to lose it's snap, or just simply gets dirty or ragged.

One of the best ways to safely clean zills is to give them a bath in ordinary ketchup. Just be sure to remove your elastic before you coat your zills, let them sit for an hour, then rince. This method is especially effective for brass finger cymbals.

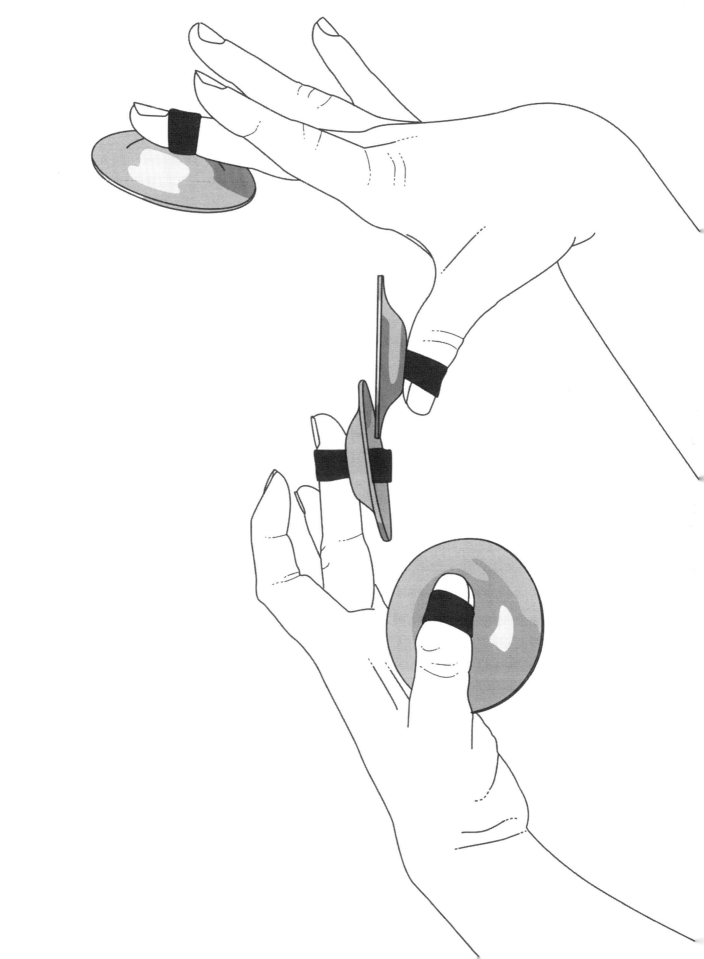

Storage: Bags and Pouches

The best way to keep your zills safe and secure is to keep them in a bag. Virtually any small bag that your zills will fit in can be used to store your zills. Bags are available in an infinite variety of styles, shapes, colors, and fabrications. So when you are shoppng for the perfect bag for your zills, here are some things to look for.

The zill bag will help keep you finger cymbals from oxidizing, and discolring. Zills that have been platedare prone to chipping especially along the edges. A zill bag will keep will also keep them together so one doesn't go slithering away into a dark corner of your dance back, or some strange location in your home.

The right size for your instruments - Look for a bag that will contain your zills, without letting them rattle around to much, but are still large enough to pull them out as needed.

A Closure you trust - No one wants to go hunting for a stray zill that's been lost at the bottom of a bag. No matter what style of bag you choose, be sure that your zills can't slither out.

Soft fabric - Make sure that the bag you choose is either made from soft, non abrasive fabric. Many dancers like to use exotic fabrics embroidered with metal or covered with mirrors, beads, and sequins. If you like a highly embellished bag, choose a version that has a soft lining to protect the finish of your instruments.

Distinctive looking - Pro-dancers and finger cymbal enthusiasts often wind up collecting a sizeable wardrobe of zills. The mission is to aquire or create a unique bag for each set so you can quickly spot the insturments you want in amongst a pile of bags.

Choose Transparent Cloth - If remembering which finger cymbals are in which bag is a challenge, you can protect your zills in organza jewelry pouches that will keep them from getting scratched, but will still allow you to visually select the perfect set.

Above: A peek into a portion of the collection of pro-dancer and teacher Sara Shrapnell.

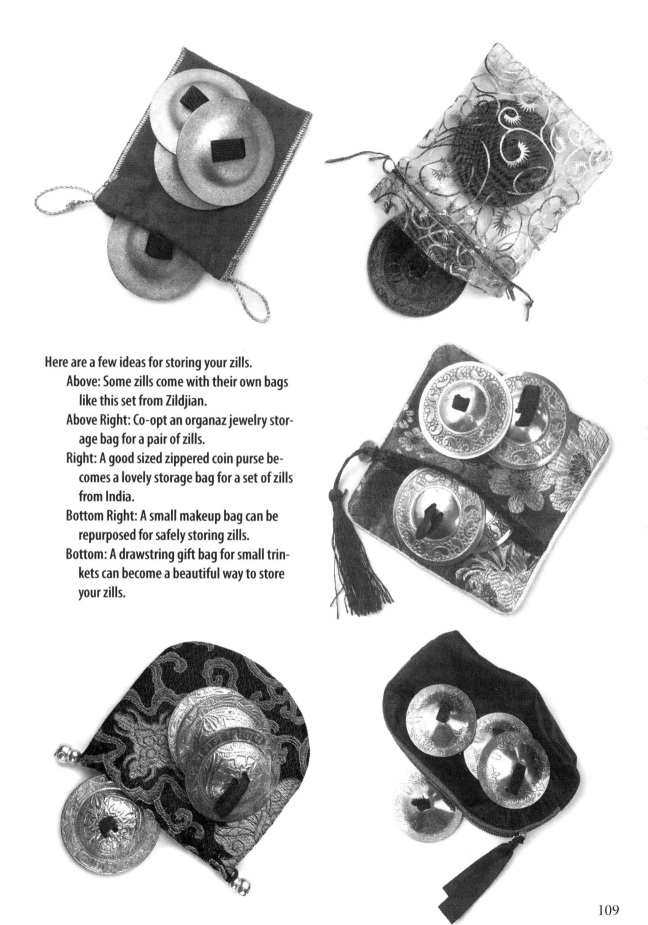

Here are a few ideas for storing your zills.

Above: Some zills come with their own bags like this set from Zildjian.

Above Right: Co-opt an organaz jewelry storage bag for a pair of zills.

Right: A good sized zippered coin purse becomes a lovely storage bag for a set of zills from India.

Bottom Right: A small makeup bag can be repurposed for safely storing zills.

Bottom: A drawstring gift bag for small trinkets can become a beautiful way to store your zills.

109

Baskets, Boxes and Trays

Organizing a large collection of zills can take ingenuity, space, and planning. Over time, your collection of zills might become one of your pride and joy, a source of pleasure to look at, and fun to pluck out a pair of cymbals to put on and dance in the moment without having to go through an unboxing or unbagging. Many dancers loves the ceremony of revealing precious zills and pulling them dramatically from a hidden place to ritualize the practice of dance.

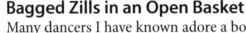

Closed Boxes

If storage in your life is a premium, or your decorating aesthetic is more clean and crisp, keeping your zill collection in a photo box, a deorative flip-top, or other closed container. This is the best storage solution for zills that are more sensitive to humidity and light like copper plated or instruments made from alloys with high copper content.

Bagged Zills in an Open Basket

Many dancers I have known adore a bohemian or ethnically inspired design aesthetic for their homes, studios, and practice spaces. If this is your style, you might choose to collect your individually bagged zill sets. Choose a basket that fits your design aesthetic and is tightly woven enough for your zills to be savely secured

Exposed Zills on a Tray

Displaying your zills on a decorative tray can create a lush and decadent display. Because they are made of metal, finger cymbals will oxidize from exposure to air. While you might enjoy wearing zills or sagat with a patina of age, you may not want your whole collection "growing old" at the same speed. If you enjoy the look of an exposed tray of zills, you can split your collection and have some on display, while others are safely protect in bags. Alternately, you could drop a piece of cloth over your tray when you aren't actively enjoying its beauty. Or you can be very strategic and aquire some lower grade zills to form the bulk of your decorative display, with only one pair of quality zills that you pick up and play as the mood strikes you.

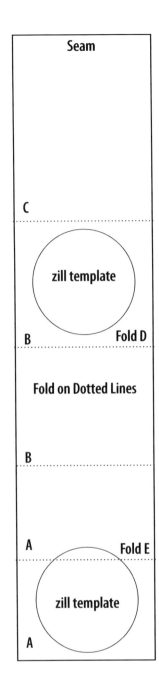

Seam

C

zill template

B   Fold D

Fold on Dotted Lines

B

A   Fold E

zill template

A

Zill Wallet

If you're interested in taking the protection and storage of your zills to the next level, why not try making a zill wallet. The basic concept is simple, create a wallet with zill-sized slots for keeping your zills from rubbing against each other. This style of zill storage will prevent your finger cymbals from scratching or even chipping the finish. This project takes very little fabric and is all composed of simple, straight line machine sewing. The real key is pressing each fold with an iron and pinning it all together to ensure that your zills fit into the pockets before you sew the entire

Pattern

Use the zills you plan on storing as your "unit" for making your pockets. Essentially, each side of the wallet is made from five zill units. In our example opposite, we made our front pocket, labelled A, slightly shorter so that I can see the edge of my zills, and know at a glance what's being stored, but you can keep it simple and make the pockets all the same size. I always recommend making a sample and putting a seam between to the two sides. Once your inner portion is stitched, use that as your pattern for the cover. This will ensure that everything aligns.

Sewing

Once your pattern is made, it's time to sew! I like to use a medium weight fusible interfacing, mounted using steam and heat, to a sturdy woven fabric. This sample is made from one fat quarter of quilting fabric. I use my sewing machine, set with a medium stitch length. I fold and press all of the pockets and top stitch 1/8" in from fold D and E. After you've completed the top stitching, press all remaining folds into place and pin. Stitch your pockets down the sides and your center seam. Before you go any further, put your zills in and test the fit. If all looks good, pin your cover to the interior, right-side to right-side. Stitch around the perimeter, leaving a gap to turn your wallet. Trim the corners and edges.

Closures

There are three main ways to keep your zill wallet closed. Snaps are my favorite method. Use a large strong snap as illustrated in the image opposite. Velcro is another great way for keeping your zills wallet closed. You can also use a button and loop closure. Round elastic and a shank button make the perfect combo for this style of closure.

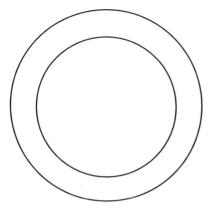

Sewn Zill Mufflers

A practical accessory to make for your finger cymbals is a set of zill mufflers. Using these on your zills allows you to reduce the volume on your practice sessions. These are great for late nights when family are asleep, folks who live in apartments and who don't want to disturb the neighbors. If you are a crafty seamstress, you can make your own set. Best of all, these are so small, you might be able to make these entirely from scraps.

Materials and Supplies

For this project you will need enough fabric to make a circle 1" larger than your favorite zills. Zill mufflers can be made from virtually any light or middle weight fabrics you have on hand. The thicker the fabric, the heavier your zills will be when you practice. This might help you build strength. You can buy or make your own bias tape. There are directions for making your bias tape in most sewing books, and there are several mentioned in the reading list. For this project, you will also need matching thread and some round elastic.

Make a pattern

Every pair of zills is slightly different in size, so on a piece of paper, trace your zill. Make a second circular line an 1 1/4" bigger from you traced line. If you have a compass laying around, it will make quick work of this step. However, you can use patience and a standard ruler to make a ring of dots. Play connect the dots to draw your line.

Cut and Sew

Once you have your pattern, cut out your four zill cozies. Using an iron for heat and steam, press your bias tape into the shape of your cozy and pin into place on the right side of the fabric. Trim your bias tape, and finish off the short edge so they abut. Next, machine stitch the the bias tape onto the cozy. Then, turn and press your bias tape to the inside and stitch down as shown in image ___. Run your round elastic through the casing you have made with the bias tape and tie, knot or stitch it down.

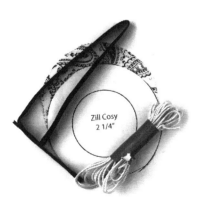

Zill Cosy
2 1/4"

Crochet Zill Mufflers

Another option to dampen the ring of your zills is to crochet a set of zill mufflers. There are many different versions and patterns for making what is essentially a set of two or four small miniature doilies that either cup the zill, or are held on by string or round elastic. The goal is to crochet a circle this is an inch bigger than your zill. You then weave a small piece of round elastic through the stitches. And that's really all there is to it.

Trace a Pattern

Trace your zill, and then draw a larger ring 1" bigger than your zill. As you work on your mini doily, refer to this pattern to ensure that your circle will reach around the lip of the zill and hold the muffler in place.

Make a Sample

I always recommend using mercerized cotton crochet thread, but any yarn will do. Because these are so small, they don't require very much yarn or thread, and don't take very much time either. Make a sample and test the fit on your zill. If it fits well enough, great! Then just go ahead and make either a mate or another pair. If it's too small or large, make any adjustments needed and make another sample until you get the fit you like.

Simple Crochet Pattern

This simple crochet pattern creates a six lobed flower pattern that uses tension to cup the zill.

This pattern utilizes cottom crochet thread with an "E" sized crochet hook. This pattern fits zills 2" - 3" in diameter depending

Starting at center, ch. 9. Join with sl st to form ring.

1st rnd: Ch 1, work 12 sc in ring. Join with sl st in 1st sc.

2nd rnd: Ch 6, skip 1st sc, sc in next sc, * ch. 5. Skip 1 sc, sc in next sc. Repeat from * (6 sps). 2 sl st up first ch to reach top of loop formed.

3rd rnd: * Ch 5, sc into next open loop. Repeat from * around. 2 sl st up first chain to reach top of loop formed.

4th rnd: * Ch 7, sc into next open loop. Repeat from * around. 3 sl st up first chain to reach top of loop formed

5th rnd: * Ch 9, sc into next open loop. Repeat from * around. 4 sl st up first chain to reach top of loop formed

6th rnd: * Ch 5, sc into next open loop. Repeat from * around. Sl st into start of first ch and tie off.

Research and References

In the next few pages, I've gathered together some of my favorite reference and resources to help you in your journey through the world of dance and finger cymbal playing. I hope that you find this section useful to you on your own personal quest for knowledge. No single book is ever fully inclusive, and for those of you who are are looking for more information the reading list is filled with excellent reference materials.

Everybody has a different path in their dance journey, and you may be a totally beginner and then grow in skill and become a huge fan of playing finger cymbals. You may be a student and are seeking supporting documentation for a research project or you might be an instructor who wants to share more information with your students.

It is virtually impossible to learn to play an instrument from a book. For those who are looking for study aids for learning to play zills, I recommend taking classes from a qualified dancer or zill player. If you do not have access to an instructor, or want to do distance study with a master, look for video recordings on line and in hard-copy DVDs. My list of video recordings is by no means exhaustive, and there are new titles coming out all the time, but the ones I have included are my favorites that I find myself recommending again and again.

Once that you have learned the basics, the only way to really get good is to practice and drill. You can play with virtually any music, but I've included some of my favorite instructional and drill CDs as a jumping off point for building your own music collection.

Zill Instructional Videos

Here is a selection of resources that are available at the time of printing. Use this resource guide as a springboard to further your own zill playing development. Videos and digital workshops are a great way to watch and learn from masters of the craft from around the world. Every instructor has their own philosophy, language, and approach to using zills in performance. I seek out and take zill playing workshops when ever I can find an instructor who is teaching. But between these opportunities I like to refresh with a digital class to inspire.

Ansuya - *Finger Cymbals with Ansuya* and *Advanced Finger Cymbals with Ansuya*

Michelle Joyce - *Killer Ziller*

Mesmera - *How to Play Finger Cymbals with Mesmera*

Karim Nagi - *Finger Cymbals: Zills & Sagat Video Instruction*

Virginia - *Learn to Play Finger Cymbals*

Z-Helene - *Finger Cymbals for the Intermediate and Advanced Dancer – Instructional Video*

Opposite: Davina plays a pair of concert sized zills with a band at a renaissance festival. When playing in large, open air areas, large zills well made zills will offer the volume and sustain that will cut through the din of conversation.

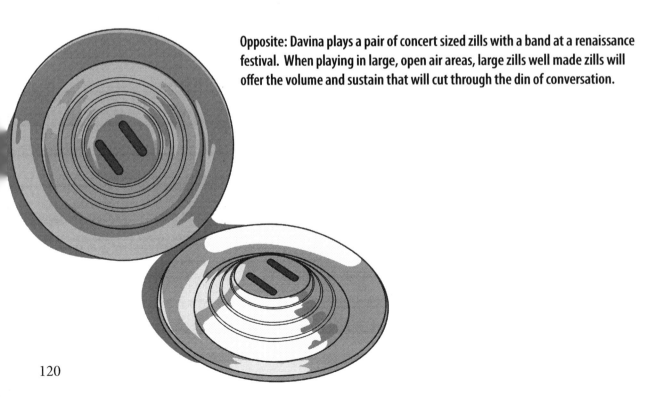

120

Music

Below is a collection of practice and instructional cd's. In this transitional time between CD's and digital downloads, be aware that these titles may be going out of print. Check with your favorite belly dance supplier to see if they

Jamilla Salimpour - ***How to Play Finger Cymbals with Jamilla***

Lily Splane – ***Zills On Fire – CD and companion book***

Mary Ellen Donald – ***Middle Eastern Rhythems 4vol CD's 2003***

Mary Ellen Donald – ***Practice Music for Drummers and Dancers***

Momo Kadous – ***The Art of Playing Finger Cymbals***

Nourhan Sharif - ***Arabic Rhythms***

Solace - ***Rhythm of Dance***

Uncle Mafufo – ***Zills and Drums: Thrilling, Chilling, Zilling***

Uncle Mafufo – ***25 Essential Rhythms for Middle Eastern Dance***

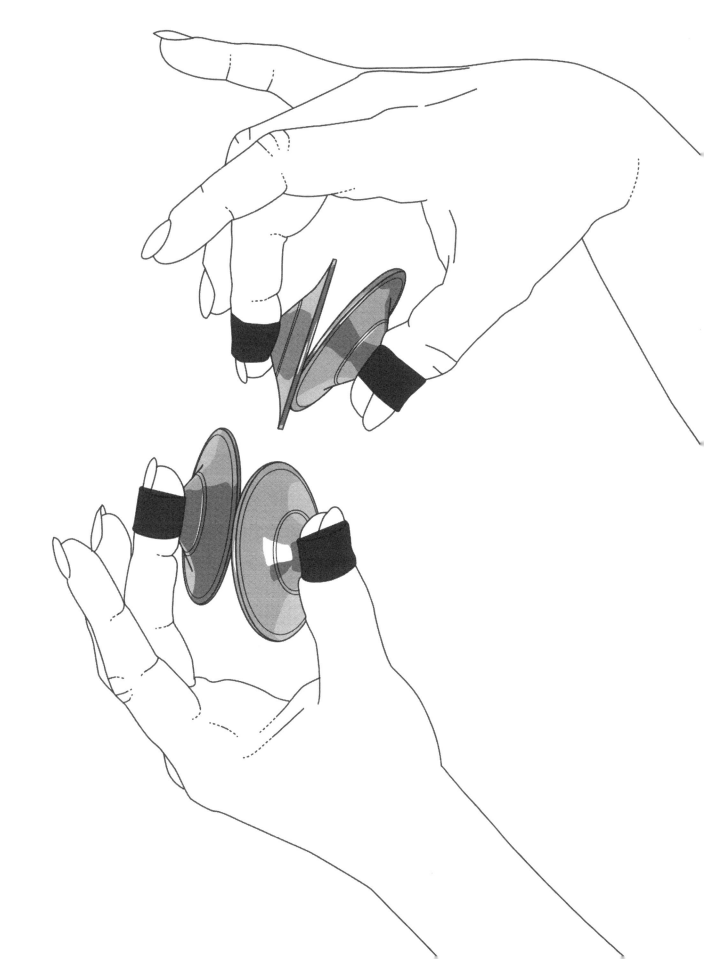

Books

The reading list is, by no means, exhaustive, but rather, a jumping off point for your to begin your own research

Cohan, Jon. *Zildjian: A History of the Legendary Cymbal Makers.* Milwaukee, WI: H. Leonard, 1999.

Cooper, Laura. *Belly Dance: Step by Step*. London: Gaia Books, 2004.

Delgado, Mimi Spencer. *Zils: The Art of Playing Finger Cymbals.* Forest Knolls, CA: Jazayer Publications, 1977.

Donald, Mary Ellen. *Mastering Finger Cymbals: Popular Belly Dance Rhythms with Suggested Dance Steps: Exercises to Strengthen Cymbal Technique, and Basic Music Theory.* San Francisco: Mary Ellen Books, 1979.

Donald, Mary Ellen. *Middle Eastern Rhythms*. San Francisco: Mary Ellen Books, 2003.

Foreman, Kelly Marie. *Zills, the Idiophone of the Middle Eastern Belly Dancer: Their History, Pedagogy, Techniques of Playing, and Role in the Context of Bodily Expression.* M.A. thesis. Kent State University, 1994.

Gilded Serpent. *The Belly Dance Reader: An Anthology of Essays*. Fairfax, CA: Gilded Serpent, 2012.

Kalani. *All About Hand Percussion.* Alfred Publishing, Co., 2008.

Petrella, Nick. *The Ultimate Guide to Cymbals.* New York: Carl Fischer, 2002.

Pinksterboer, Hugo and Rick Mattingly. *The Cymbal Book.* Milwaukee, WI: Hal Leonard Pub. Corp., 1992.

Salimpour, Jamila. A*n Illustrated Maual of Finger Cymbal Instruction*. Salimpour: Berkeley, 1977

Sharif, Keti. Bellydance: *A Guide to Middle Eastern Dance; It's Music, It's Culture and Costume.* Crow's Next, Australia: Allen & Unwin, 2004.

Woods, Jenna. *The Dancing Cymbalist: How to Play Music with Finger Cymbals and Dance at the Same Time.* Boulder, CO: Onya Music in Motion Arts, 2007.

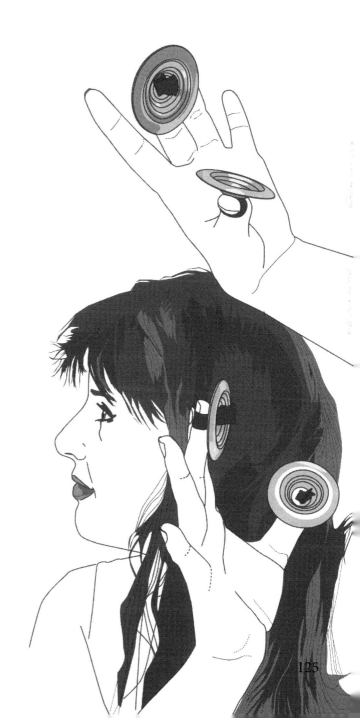

Special Thanks

Saroyan Mastercrafts

We had the opportunity to visit the Saroyan Mastercrafts factory and learn how zills are made. Vincent, the new owner is kind, smart, and forward thinking and has taken this hand craft to the next level with modern precision machining. He demonstrated the process step-by-step from metal to musical instrument. I've been a huge, long-time collector of Saroyan Zills and highly recommend that every dancer try at least one pair of Saroyan finger cymbals. Visit their website to hear sound clips of all of their products. www.saroyancymbals.com

Michael Baxter

Zills: Music on Your Fingertips began it's life as a class hand-out in 2003 and evolved into a small 40 page booklet in 2005. Photographer Michael Baxter helped me create the initial photos for that publication, including product shots of zills and many-many images of my hands. Over the intervening years, Michael's career as a belly dance photographer has taken off and he's gone on to take photos of dancers all around the world. His work is on thousands of websites, numerous publications, and a fat stack of DVD covers! I'm very happy to include some of his early, unpublished work in this book. The following photos from him from the original version, and look forward to working with him on my next book project.

BellyDance.com

This is a special shout out to Mher and his team over at Bellydance.com, who helped me track down the music and video resources that helped make the reference section of this book as complete as possible. www.bellydance.com

Artemis Imports

Yolanda over at Artemis Imports was extremely helpful in hunting down some older, out of print books and cd's. I also picked up several pairs of student and pro grade zills from her store. Over the many years I've been performing, teaching and writing books, I've lots of wonderful jewelry and costume pieces, and have always had wonderful service. artemisimports.com

Nancy Hernandez

One of my mentors in belly dance, Nancy Hernandez, textile historian and collector, and belly dance scholar. Her advice was key in shaping the direction and scope of this book, and it's a much richer publication because of help and insights in the content, organization, and structure.

Amanda

When I was looking for specific information about the various concussion idiophones, I decided to call in our local expert on the topic Amanda. She is truly a community leader here in the greater San Francisco/San Jose area hosting workshops, teaching classes, and sharing outstanding performances at community events. She taught me how to hold and play Turkish spoons, and without her knowledge and patience as a teacher, this book wouldn't be as complete. For more information visit her website amandadancer.com

Sara Shrapnell

I would like to take a moment to thank my fellow author and co-conspirator, Sara Shrapnell of letsbellydanceusa.com for providing a thoughtful sounding board for the ideas that coalesced into this book. I worked on this book Zills as we finished up our collaborative book project, "Becoming a Belly Dancer: From Student to Stage," with Poppy Maya and Alisha Westerfeld. Over the summer of 2016, I was flip-flopping between projects and she patiently helped me edit this book, as we were editing that book. I couldn't have survived without her help!

Joe Devine

I was able to do a great deal of fact checking on metallurgy, precision machining, and industrial technology from my brother Joe. His knowledge and expertise was essential for making the sections on ancient and modern technology of metal working and finger cymbal construction complete. Thanks bro - Love you man!

About the team

Dawn Devine ~ Davina

With over 20 books published in as many years, Dawn Devine aka Davina is a professional belly dance costume designer, performer, and instructor. Through her writings on her blog and in books she is on a mission to help DIY minded dancers make beautiful, well fitting, and durable belly dance costumes. You can find out more about Dawn and her books and current projects on her website. www.davina.us

Alisha Westerfeld ~ Zemira - Photographer

Photography is an ongoing, lifelong passion for Alisha. In the "All About" series of books from Ibexa Press, Alisha has had the opportunity to marry her skills in photography, with her loves of dance, beautiful costumes, and performance art. In addition to The Cloth of Egypt: All About Assiut, and Zills, she worked as part of the team who created the book Becoming a Belly Dancer: From Student to Stage. When she is not taking photos of beautiful belly dancers, she enjoys nature and travel photography. See more of her work on her digital gallery: alishawesterfeld.smugmug.com

George Goncalves - Illustrator

George's work in Zills is a mirror of the eclectic mix of the artists and images that have fascinated him since childhood. In it are hints ligne claire, fumetti, and the vibrant illustration style of the 50's and 60's. The theater, and performance in general, has also long been a source of inspiration, often explored through a variety of computer arts techniques, of which he took full advantage in this project. This is his first collaboration with Ibexa Press.

Our Models

Basinah
www.basinahdances.com

Chaise

Poppy Maya
www.poppymaya.co.uk

redvelvet gold

Sara Shrapnell
letsbellydanceusa.com

Shalimar

Thank you to our family and friends in the dance community who have joined us for this project. Alisha and I had such a great time working with these ladies on this and other projects and look forward to working with you on many more projects in the future!

Dawn Devine ~ Davina

Left: Dawn Devine aka Davina wearing assiut

More Books by Dawn Devine

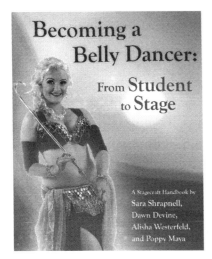

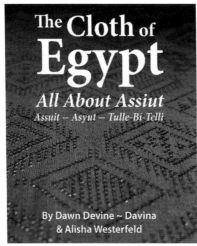

Becoming a Belly Dancer: From Student to Stage, a Stagecraft handbook for students and performers. This 402 page book contains over 1000 photos to illustrate the informative and inspirational text that helps you take your belly dance performance preperation and presentation to the next level. From choosing an instructor to going pro, and everything in between, there's tons of information for belly dancers of all levels. With Sara Shrapnell, Poppy Maya, and Alisha Westerfeld.

The Cloth of Egypt: All About Assiut is the culmination of more than 20 years of research on the subject of this magical cloth. No matter how you spell it, this single stitch metal embroidery technique has a fascinating history, enhanced by a host of legends and lore. Broken down into four major sections, it addresses the history, technology, wearing, and uses for this wonderful cloth. With photography by Alisha Westerfeld

Embellished Bras - Basic Techniques is the international best selling book on making your own custom belly dance bra, From draping your bra base, to the final decoration,

This book accompanies Davina's workshop/lecture of the same name where she demonstrates how she can quickly make a custom pattern for any bra using professional draping techniques. With photography by Barry Brown

---

Visit Davina's website to get a free copy
of Hints & Tips and sign up for her mailing list
for a printable coloring book.

www.davina.us

Skirting the Issues and Pants for the Dance combines volumes 2 and 3 of Dawn Devine's Belly Dance Costume Essentials series into a single edition. Designed for dancers, designers, and costume makers, this book offers hundreds of ideas, tips and hints for crafting original, beautiful and well-constructed garments. This book is lavishly illustrated with instructions for how to take your body measurements and draft your own custom fit patterns.

From Turban to Toe Ring explores the various layers and elements that compose the tribal style costume. From jewelry and cosmetics to cholis, skirts, and pants, this book is loaded with directions for designing and making the garments described in the book. With over 300 illustrations and step-by-step diagrams, this book is an essential addition to the reference libraries of costumers, teachers, and tribal style dancers. Not just for costumers, it also contains costume parts and pieces that can be used to make ensembles suitable for dancers who just want a more folkloric, historical, fusion, or Gypsy look.

Bedlah, Baubles and Beads is the book that focusses exclusively on the "cabaret" style so common in the United States and around the world. It is specifically about designing and crafting the elaborate bra and belt sets, or bedlah, worn by belly dancers at all levels of their dance journey from student to professional. Contains hundreds of tips, hints, and directions for making contemporary belly dance costumes.

Costuming From the Hip is the book that started it all. The comprehensive reference for all types of Middle Eastern dance costuming. Dancers, costume makers, designers, and historical re-enactors will like the over 200 illustrations, historical patterns, construction techniques, and hundreds of hints and tips. This book will take you step by step through measuring your body, researching your costume, laying out the patterns, fitting it, and accessorizing your creation.

Made in the USA
San Bernardino, CA
14 October 2016